T0255245

Python Unit Test Automation

Automate, Organize, and Execute Unit Tests in Python

Second Edition

Ashwin Pajankar

Apress®

Python Unit Test Automation: Automate, Organize, and Execute
Unit Tests in Python

Ashwin Pajankar
Nashik, Maharashtra, India

ISBN-13 (pbk): 978-1-4842-7853-6   ISBN-13 (electronic): 978-1-4842-7854-3
https://doi.org/10.1007/978-1-4842-7854-3

Copyright © 2022 by Ashwin Pajankar

Managing Director, Apress Media LLC: Welmoed Spahr
Acquisitions Editor: Celestin Suresh John
Development Editor: James Markham
Coordinating Editor: Mark Powers
Copyeditor: Kezia Endsley

Cover designed by eStudioCalamar

Cover image by Jason Leung on Unsplash (www.unsplash.com)

Distributed to the book trade worldwide by Apress Media, LLC, 1 New York Plaza, New York, NY 10004, U.S.A. Phone 1-800-SPRINGER, fax (201) 348-4505, e-mail orders-ny@springer-sbm.com, or visit www.springeronline.com. Apress Media, LLC is a California LLC and the sole member (owner) is Springer Science + Business Media Finance Inc (SSBM Finance Inc). SSBM Finance Inc is a **Delaware** corporation.

For information on translations, please e-mail booktranslations@springernature.com; for reprint, paperback, or audio rights, please e-mail bookpermissions@springernature.com.

Apress titles may be purchased in bulk for academic, corporate, or promotional use. eBook versions and licenses are also available for most titles. For more information, reference our Print and eBook Bulk Sales web page at http://www.apress.com/bulk-sales.

Any source code or other supplementary material referenced by the author in this book is available to readers on GitHub. For more detailed information, please visit http://www.apress.com/source-code.

Printed on acid-free paper

I dedicate this book to Alan Mathison Turing, an English mathematician, computer scientist, logician, cryptanalyst, and philosopher who was influential in the development of theoretical computer science.

Table of Contents

About the Author

Ashwin Pajankar is a programmer, a maker, an author, a YouTuber, and a science popularizer. He graduated from IIIT Hyderabad with an MTech in Computer Science and Engineering. He has a keen interest in promoting science, technology, engineering, and mathematics (STEM) education. He has written many books with Packt, Leanpub, BPB, and Apress, and has also reviewed many books for Packt and Apress. He's also working on many more books with Apress.

His YouTube channel has more than 10,000 subscribers and he also teaches more than 75,000 students on Udemy.

His personal website is `www.AshwinPajankar.com`.

His LinkedIn profile is
`https://in.linkedin.com/in/ashwinpajankar`

About the Technical Reviewers

Shraddha Joshi is currently working as an engineer at PwC with experience in testing with Python and Java in major production environments. She has worked with various global clients across multiple domains and helped them build products and solutions with full-fledged testing frameworks. She has expertise in all phases of the development process and leads the design, development, execution, and automation stages of test plans for a diverse set of system components. Previously, she was a Senior Quality Engineer at Incture Technologies, where she was involved in designing functional integration and regression test plans, building and executing manual and automated tests, and performing highly complex analysis for multiple products. She also helped set cross-functional product testing standards involving the application of advanced technical/business skills in the area of specialization.

Shraddha's great knack for simplifying concepts and explaining them in an easy-to-understand manner makes her stand apart. She is passionate about guiding and mentoring people in their technology journey. She is also actively involved in conducting workshops, webinars, and sessions.

She lives in Bangalore with her family.

Sujay Raghavendra is a distinguished IT professional with a master's degree in Information Technology. His research interests include computer vision, NLP, machine learning, deep learning, and artificial intelligence. He has served as an advisor for various universities and startups. He has been active in the research community. He has also authored a book with Apress Media. He has published research papers at various international journals and conferences and is a leading industry expert and mentor for professionals.

Acknowledgments

I am grateful to the student and teacher community which, with their continual bombardment of queries, impelled me to learn more, simplify my findings, and organize them into a book. This book is for them.

I wish to thank my friends and colleagues—the practitioners from the field—for their good counsel and for filling me in on the latest in the field of test automation.

A special thanks to the technical reviewers—Shraddha and Sujay—for their vigilant review and for providing their expert opinions.

I consider myself very fortunate for the editorial assistance provided by Apress; the collaboration with them has been fabulous. I am thankful to Celestin Suresh John, Senior Manager, Editorial Acquisitions, Apress and Springer Science and Business Media Company, for giving me this and many other opportunities to collaborate with Apress. I wish to acknowledge and appreciate James Markham, Mark Powers, and the team of associates from Apress who adeptly guided me through the entire process of preparation and publication.

Introduction

Why This Book?

I have been using Python for more than ten years on a wide variety of projects. Initially, I used it for GUI applications. Then I quickly moved to scientific usage, as my academic projects demanded it. When I entered professional life, I used it for automation first and then for implementation of alert mechanisms. I have been using Python for the last six years in the fields of scientific computing, Internet of Things (IoT), and single board computers. I have written plenty of Python code over these years.

I always prefer it to bash scripting, which offers limited capabilities to users like me. At different points over the last ten years, I've worked as a developer, an R&D engineer, a maker, an author, and a QA specialist. I used Python in every single role.

Whenever I write code, I unit test it thoroughly. I used to unit test all my Python modules in the good old manual way. I used to run all the scripts once and compare the outcome with what was expected. However, I learned that when your codebase grows larger, it's pretty difficult to test the scripts manually. Also, all the scripts have to be tested, re-tested, and tested for regression whenever a small part of the codebase changes. I was looking for a way to run all the tests automatically, which led me to reading about test automation. It immediately piqued my curiosity and, after a couple of days, I was running my own automated Python tests.

After acquainting myself with the philosophy of test automation, I applied my newfound knowledge to automate unit and integration testing to web, mobile, GUI, API, and a variety of other types of applications using programming languages like C++, Python, Java, and PHP.

I wrote this book to share my knowledge and experiences while automating unit tests in Python 3. I explore different frameworks and plugins in this book. I learned about the tools and techniques explained in this book by spending numerous hours learning, coding, discussing, and actively participating in diverse Internet forums. I have condensed the knowledge to the basics of the unit test automation frameworks. I hope you will enjoy reading and following the book as much as I enjoyed writing it. This book includes the following:

- An introduction to Python and various IDEs

- Various test automation frameworks for Python 3, including `doctest`, `unittest`, `nose`, `nose2`, and `pytest`

- Logging frameworks and web driver automation

- Coding standards for Python 3 test automation and implementation of test-driven development with `pytest` in Python 3

Who This Book Is For

The main audience of this book is Python 3 programmers who want to automate their unit tests. This includes a large and diverse set of people, including developers, test automators, students, researchers, and novice learners. The book is for those who have some knowledge of the Python programming language. The test automation engineers who have already worked with other programming frameworks, such as Java and C++, will find this book immensely useful to learn how test automation is done in Python 3. If you are just beginning with Python 3 programming and want to quickly get into automating the unit tests of your modules and packages, you will find this book helpful.

This book is *not* a book for learning Python 3 programming and syntax from scratch. It is also not a DIY cookbook for development projects. If your understanding of coding is limited, you will find it difficult to follow this book.

How This Book Is Organized

This book has eight chapters. Here is a sneak peek into the topics covered in each chapter:

- **Chapter 1:** This chapter introduces you to the history and philosophy of Python. It teaches you how to install Python and how to set up the environment for Python 3 programming. It also briefly explores the new features of Python 3 and introduces you to a few popular Python 3 IDEs.

- **Chapter 2:** The aim of this chapter is to quickly get you started with unit test automation in Python 3. The chapter revises the understanding of testing concepts and quickly moves into implementing those concepts with docstring and doctest.

- **Chapter 3:** This chapter serves to introduce xUnit and its philosophy to you. Then it proceeds to teach you how to implement concepts of xUnit with unittest, a xUnit port for Python.

- **Chapter 4:** This chapter explores the inadequacies of unittest. Then it explores a better unit-testing framework, called nose. It explains the installation of plugins for nose to generate reports. It also discusses nose2, which is nose's next-generation version that's under active development.

- **Chapter 5:** This chapter introduces you to a modular, easy-to-use, unit test framework for Python, called `pytest`. It discusses the drawbacks of `nose` and compares `nose`, `unittest`, and `pytest`.

- **Chapter 6:** This chapter introduces you to a web driver automation framework known as `selenium`. You will learn how to use the Selenium IDE and Selenium Python library.

- **Chapter 7:** This chapter introduces you to various logging frameworks in Python. First, you will explore the built-in framework, `logging`. Then you will explore a third-party logging library, called `loguru`.

- **Chapter 8:** This chapter helps you understand the coding and filenaming conventions for facilitating easier test discovery across various unit test frameworks in Python. The chapter concludes the book by implementing a test-driven development in Python 3 using `pytest`.

How to Get the Most Out of This Book

To get the most out of this book, it's best to abide by the following:

- Read the chapters thoroughly. Use the chapters hands-on by following the step-by-step instructions stated in the code examples. Do not skip any of the code examples.

- If need be, repeat them a second time or until the concept is firmly etched in your mind.

- Join a Python community or discussion forum.

- Explore and practice with various Python IDEs

- Read the online documentation available for various test automation frameworks for Python 3.

- Read the blogs related to test automation, Python 3, migration to Python 3 from Python 2, logging, and test-driven development.

Where Next?

I have endeavored to unleash the power of the unit test automation libraries for Python 3 as an aid to the community of professional developers and testers. I recommend you read the book from cover to cover, without skipping any of the chapters, text, or code examples.

I wish you well in exploring Python!

A Quick Word About the Instructors' Fraternity

Attention has been paid to the sequence of chapters and to the flow of topics in each chapter. This is done particularly with an objective to assist my fellow instructors and academicians in carving out a syllabus from the Table of Contents (ToC) of the book. The complete ToC complements the syllabus of "Introduction to Software Testing," if students were introduced to programming during their freshman year with the help of Python.

I have ensured that each concept discussed in this book includes adequate hands-on content to enable you to teach better and to provide ample hands-on practice to your students.

Happy learning and exploring!

—Ashwin Pajankar

CHAPTER 1

Introduction to Python

I hope you have glanced through the introduction section. If you have not, then I recommend reading it, as it will help you with the context and the philosophy of this book.

Let's begin this adventurous journey by learning the history and background of Python.

I personally find Python amazing and have been enchanted by it. Python is a simple yet powerful programming language. When using Python, it's easy to focus on the implementation of the solution to a given problem, as programmers do not have to worry about the syntax of the programming language.

The History of Python

Python was conceived in the late 1980s. Guido van Rossum began its implementation in late 1989 at the Centrum Wiskunde & Informatica (National Research Institute for Mathematics and Computer Science) in the Netherlands. Python is a successor to the ABC programming language, which itself was inspired by SETL. In February 1991, Van Rossum published Python code to the `alt.sources` newsgroup. The name Python was inspired by the television show "Monty Python's Flying Circus," as Van Rossum is a big fan of Monty Python.

© Ashwin Pajankar 2022
A. Pajankar, *Python Unit Test Automation*, https://doi.org/10.1007/978-1-4842-7854-3_1

Van Rossum is the principal author of Python. He played a central role in guiding the development and evolution of Python. He held the title of *Benevolent Dictator for Life* for Python. In 2018, he stepped down from that role. As of the writing of this edition, he works for Microsoft.

The central philosophy of Python, called the *Zen of Python,* is explained in PEP-20, which can be found at `https://www.python.org/dev/peps/pep-0020`.

It is a collection of 20 software principles, as follows:

- Beautiful is better than ugly.

- Explicit is better than implicit.

- Simple is better than complex.

- Complex is better than complicated.

- Flat is better than nested.

- Sparse is better than dense.

- Readability counts.

- Special cases aren't special enough to break the rules.

- Practicality beats purity.

- Errors should never pass silently.

- Unless explicitly silenced.

- In the face of ambiguity, refuse the temptation to guess.

- There should be one—and preferably only one— obvious way to do it.

- Although that way may not be obvious at first unless you're Dutch.

- Now is better than never.

- Although never is often better than right now.

- If the implementation is hard to explain, it's a bad idea.

- If the implementation is easy to explain, it may be a good idea.

- Namespaces are one honking great idea—let's do more of those!

Features of Python

The following sections discuss the features of Python that have become popular and beloved in the programming community.

Simple

Python is a simple and minimalist language. Reading a well written and good Python program makes you feel as if you are reading English text.

Easy to Learn

Due to its simple and English-like syntax, Python is extremely easy for beginners to learn.

That is the prime reason that, nowadays, it is taught as the first programming language to high school and university students who take introduction to programming and programming 101 courses. An entire new generation of programmers is learning Python as their first programming language.

Easy to Read

Unlike other high-level programming languages, Python does not provide much provision for obfuscating code and making it unreadable. The English-like structure of Python code makes it easier to read, compared to code written in other programming languages. This makes it easier to understand and easier to learn, compared to other high-level languages like C and C++.

Easy to Maintain

As Python code is easy to read, easy to understand, and easy to learn, anyone maintaining the code becomes comfortable with its codebase in considerably less time. I can vouch for this from personal experiences of maintaining and enhancing large legacy codebases written in a combination of bash and Python 2.

Open Source

Python is an open-source project. That means its source code is freely available. You can make changes to it to suit your needs and use the original and changed code in your applications.

High-Level Language

While writing Python programs, you do not have to manage low-level details like memory management, CPU timings, and scheduling processes. All these tasks are managed by the Python interpreter. You can directly write the code in easy-to- understand, English-like syntax.

Portable

Python has been ported to many platforms. All Python programs work on any of these platforms without requiring any changes, if you are careful enough to avoid any system-dependent features. You can use Python on GNU/Linux, Windows, Android, FreeBSD, macOS, iOS, Solaris, OS/2, Amiga, AROS, AS/400, BeOS, OS/390, z/OS, Palm OS, QNX, VMS, Psion, Acorn, RISC OS, VxWorks, PlayStation, Sharp Zaurus, Windows CE, and PocketPC.

Interpreted

Python is an interpreted language. Programs written in a high-level programming language like C, C++, and Java are first compiled. This means that they are first converted into an intermediate format. When you run the program, this intermediate format is loaded from secondary storage (i.e., a hard disk) to memory (RAM) by the linker/loader. So, C, C++, and Java have separate compilers and linkers/loaders. This is not the case with Python. Python runs its programs directly from the source code. You do not have to bother about compiling and linking to the proper libraries. This makes Python programs truly portable, as you can copy the program to one computer from another and the program runs fine as long as the necessary libraries are installed on the target computer.

Object-Oriented

Python supports object-oriented programming paradigms. In object-oriented programming languages, the program is built around objects that combine data and related functionality. Python is a very simple but powerful object-oriented programming language.

Extensible

One of the features of Python is that you can call C and C++ routines from Python programs. If you want the core functionality of the application to run faster, you can code that part in C/C++ and call it in the Python program (C/C++ programs generally run faster than Python).

Extensive Libraries

Python has an extensive standard library, which comes pre-installed. The standard library has all the essential features of a modern day programming language. It has provision for databases, unit testing (we will explore this in this book), regular expressions, multi-threading, network programming, computer graphics, image processing, GUI, and other utilities. This is part of Python's *batteries-included* philosophy.

Apart from standard library, Python has a large and ever-growing set of third-party libraries. The list of these libraries can be found in the Python Package Index (`https://pypi.org/`). We will explore a few libraries like `unittest`, `nose`, `nose2`, `pytest`, and `selenium` for test automation in this book. I also have worked with and extensively written on the libraries for scientific computing and computer vision such as `numpy`, `scipy`, `matplotlib`, `pillow`, `scikit-image`, and OpenCV.

Robust

Python provides robustness by means of its ability to handle errors. The full stack trace of the encountered errors is available and makes the programmer's life more bearable. The runtime errors are known as *exceptions*. The feature that allows handling of these errors is known as the *exception handling mechanism*.

Rapid Prototyping

Python is used as a *rapid prototyping tool*. As you have read, Python has extensive libraries and is easy to learn, so many software architects are increasingly using it as a tool to rapidly prototype their ideas into working models in a very short period of time.

Memory Management

In assembly language and programming languages like C and C++, memory management is the responsibility of the programmer. And this is in addition to the task at hand. This creates an unnecessary burden on the programmer. In Python, the Python interpreter handles memory management. This helps programmers steer clear of memory issues and focus on the task at hand.

Powerful

Python has everything in it for a modern programming language. It is used for applications like computer vision, supercomputing, drug discovery, scientific computing, simulation, and bioinformatics. Millions of programmers around the world use Python. Many big organizations like NASA, Google, SpaceX, and Cisco use Python for their applications and infrastructure.

Community Support

I find this the most appealing feature of Python. As you have read, Python is open source and has a community of almost a million programmers (probably more, as today's high school kids are learning Python) throughout the world. That means there are plenty of forums on the Internet supporting programmers who encounter roadblocks. None of my queries related to Python has ever gone unanswered.

Python 3

Python 3 was released in 2008. The Python development team decided to do away with some of the redundant features of the Python language, simplify some of its features, rectify some design flaws, and add some much-needed features.

It was decided that a major revision number was warranted and the resultant release would not be backward compatible. Python 2.x and 3.x were supposed to coexist in parallel for the programmer community to have enough time to migrate their code and the third-party libraries from 2.x to 3.x. Python 2.x code cannot run on Python 3 in many cases, as there are significant differences between 2.x and 3.x.

Differences Between Python 2 and Python 3

The following are the most notable differences between Python 2 and Python 3. Let's look at them in brief:

- The `print()` function

  This is perhaps the most notable difference between Python 2 and Python 3. The `print` statement of Python 2 is replaced with the `print()` function in Python 3.

- Integer division

  The nature of integer division has been changed in
  Python 3 for the sake of mathematical correctness.
  In Python 2, the result of division of two integer
  operands is an integer. However, in Python 3, it is a
  float value.

- Omission of `xrange()`

  In Python 2, for creating iterable objects, the
  `xrange()` function is used. In Python 3, `range()` is
  implemented much like `xrange()`. So, a separate
  `xrange()` is not needed anymore. Using `xrange()` in
  Python 3 raises a `nameError`.

- Raising exceptions

  It is mandatory in Python 3 to enclose exception
  arguments, if any, in parentheses, whereas in
  Python 2 it is optional.

- Handling exceptions

  In Python 3, while handling exceptions, the `as`
  keyword is needed before the parameter to handle
  an argument. In Python 2, it is not needed.

- New style classes

  Python 2 supports old and new style classes,
  whereas Python 3 supports only new style classes.
  All classes created in Python 3 use new style classes
  by default.

- New features of Python 3

  The following new features of Python 3 have not
  been backported to Python 2:

  a.   Strings are Unicode by default

  b.   Clean Unicode/byte separation

  c.   Exception chaining

  d.   Function annotations

  e.   Syntax for keyword-only arguments

  f.   Extended tuple unpacking

  g.   Non-local variable declarations

From this list, you will be frequently using `print()`, new-style classes,
and exceptions in the code examples in this book.

Why Use Python 3

From the previous list, you will be frequently using new-style classes and
exceptions in the code examples in this book.

Python's wiki page (`https://wiki.python.org/moin/`
`Python2orPython3`) says the following:

> *Python 3 is strongly recommended for any new development.*

New generation of programmers are introduced to Python 3 as their
first programming language. When they are comfortable with the concept
and philosophy of Python programming, they are gradually introduced
to Python 2 so that they can also work with legacy codebases. Many
organizations have already started migrating codebases from Python 2 to
Python 3. All new projects in Python extensively use Python 3. Python 2 is
almost dead as of writing of this edition of the book. Most organizations
are migrating their legacy codebases from Python 2 to Python 3. Day by

day, there is less and less code in Python 2 and it is either abandoned or converted to Python 3. It is a long and tedious process to convert Python 2 code to Python 3. Many organizations are doing it on as-needed basis. The general rule of thumb that most organizations follow is that if the code works then they do not touch it. However, as I have already said, all the new projects involving Python are kicked off with Python 3. Going forward, conversion of legacy Python 2 codebase to Python 3 will present technically challenging and financially lucrative opportunities for professionals.

I personally think that these are pretty good reasons to use Python 3.

Installing Python 3

This section discusses how to install Python 3 on various commonly used computer OSs.

Installation on Linux

Linux has many popular distributions. Python 3 is preinstalled on many popular distributions.

Installation on Debian, Ubuntu, and Derivatives

The Python 3 interpreter comes preinstalled on the latest releases of Debian, Ubuntu, and their derivatives.

Installation on Fedora and CentOS

The Python 3 interpreter comes preinstalled on the latest releases of Fedora and CentOS.

> **Note**   On most of the latest Linux distributions, both versions
> of Python (Python 2 and Python 3) are installed by default. The
> interpreter for Python 2 is a binary executable file named `python` and
> the interpreter for Python 3 is another binary executable file named
> `python3`. You can use `python3 --V` or `python3 --version` to
> check the version of the Python 3 interpreter installed on your Linux
> computer. Also, you can use the `which python3` command to
> determine the location of the interpreter on the disk.

Installation on macOS X

On macOS X, the Python 2 interpreter is installed by default and can be
invoked from the terminal using the `python` command. If you want to use
Python 3, you have to install it. Make sure that the computer is connected
to the Internet and run the `brew install python3` command in the
terminal. This will install Python 3. It will also install other utilities, such as
`pip`, `setuptools`, and `wheel`.

   Once the installation finishes, go to the terminal and type `python3 --V`
or `python3 --version` to check the version of the Python 3 interpreter
installed.

Installation on Windows

In Windows OS, Python 3 installation requires a bit more effort. Python 2
or Python 3 is not preinstalled on a Windows computer. In order to
install it, you have to visit the downloads section of the Python website at
`https://www.python.org/downloads`, as shown in Figure 1-1.

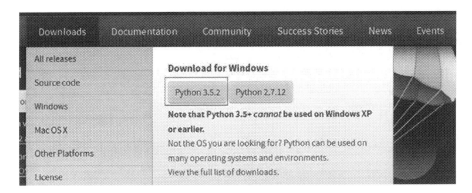

Figure 1-1. *Python downloads section on the website*

Select Python 3.5.2. (The numbers 5 and 2 might change if there is a new stable release of Python after the book is published.) This will download the setup file for Python 3. Open the setup file once it is downloaded. Click on the Run button in the dialog box shown in Figure 1-2.

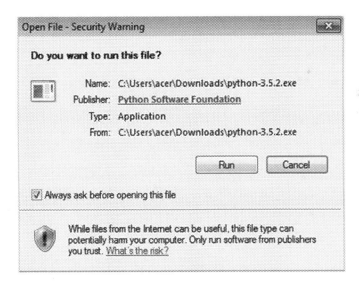

Figure 1-2. *Open File - Security Warning dialog box*

13

Note   Depending on the settings, you might require admin privileges to install Python 3 (or any other program, for that matter) on a Windows computer. If you are in an organizational setting, check with your system admin team for this information.

If you are using Windows 7, depending on the update status of your computer, you might encounter the message box shown in Figure 1-3.

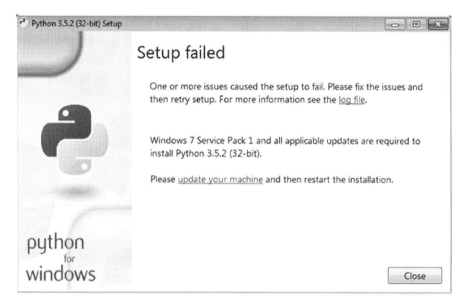

Figure 1-3. *Setup Failed message for Windows 7*

Update the OS by installing any Windows updates and then rerun the setup file. The window in Figure 1-4 will appear when you are successful.

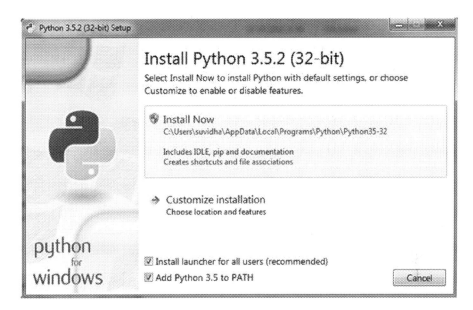

Figure 1-4. *Python Installation window*

Check the Add Python 3.x to PATH checkbox. This will ensure that Python is added to the PATH system variable and you will be able to access Python from the command prompt of Windows (cmd) after the installation. Click the Install Now button and continue the setup wizard. Once installation finishes, it will show a success message.

Running a Python Program and Python Modes

You have set up your environment for Python programming now. Now you can get started with a simple concept of Python. Python has two basic modes—normal and interactive. Let's look at these modes in detail.

Interactive Mode

Python's interactive mode is a command-line shell that provides immediate output for every executed statement. It also stores the output of previously executed statements in active memory. As new statements are executed by the Python interpreter, the entire sequence of previously executed statements is considered while evaluating the current output. You have to type python3 in the command prompt of Linux/macOS and python in the command prompt cmd of Windows to invoke the Python 3 interpreter into interactive mode, as follows:

```
Python 3.4.2 (default, Oct 19 2014, 13:31:11)
[GCC 4.9.1] on linux
Type "help", "copyright", "credits" or "license" for more
information.
>>>
```

You can execute Python statements directly in this interactive mode just like you run commands in the OS shell/console, as follows:

```
>>> print('Hello World!')
Hello World!
>>>
```

You will not be using interactive mode in the book. However, it's the quickest way to check small snippets of code (5 to 10 lines). You can quit interactive mode with the exit() statement, as follows:

```
>>> exit()
$
```

Script Mode

Script mode is where the Python script files (.py) are executed by the Python interpreter.

Create a file called test.py and add the print ('Hello World!') statement to the file. Save the file and run it with the Python 3 interpreter as follows.

```
$ python3 test.py
Hello World!
$
```

In this example, python3 is the interpreter and test.py is the filename. If the Python test.py file is not in the same directory where you're invoking the python3 interpreter, you have to provide the absolute path of the Python file.

Note   For all Linux and Mac computers, the command for the Python 3 interpreter is python3. For Windows, it is just python, assuming that only Python 3 is installed on the Windows computer and its location is added to the PATH variable during installation or manually after the installation. Throughout this book, I use a Linux command prompt (on my Raspberry Pi 4) to run the code examples. I will mention it explicitly wherever Windows is used for a couple of examples.

IDEs for Python

An Integrated Development Environment (IDE) is a software suite that has all the basic tools to write and test programs. A typical IDE has a compiler, a debugger, a code editor, and a build automation tool. Most programming languages have various IDEs to make programmers lives better. Python too has many IDEs. Let's take a look at a few IDEs for Python.

IDLE

IDLE stands for Integrated Development Environment. It comes bundled with Python. IDLE3 is for Python 3. It's popular with beginners of Python. Just type idle3 in the command prompt in a Linux computer where Python 3 is installed. Figure 1-5 is a screenshot of an IDLE3 code editor and an interactive prompt.

Figure 1-5. *IDLE3 running on a Raspberry Pi*

If IDLE is not installed by default on your Linux distribution then you have to install it manually. For Debian and derivatives, the command for the installation is as follows:

```
sudo apt-get install idle
```

The PyDev Plugin for Eclipse

If you are a seasoned Java programmer, you probably have worked on Eclipse. Eclipse is a very popular IDE for Java and it can be used with other programming languages too. PyDev is a Python IDE for Eclipse, and it can be used in Python, Jython, and IronPython development (see Figure 1-6). You can install PyDev from the Eclipse marketplace at www.pydev.org.

19

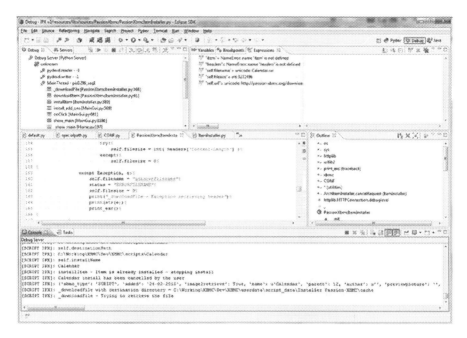

Figure 1-6. *Eclipse with PyDev*

Geany

Geany (see Figure 1-7) is a text editor that uses the GTK+ toolkit with basic features of an integrated development environment. It supports many file types and has some nice features. Check out `https://www.geany.org` for more details.

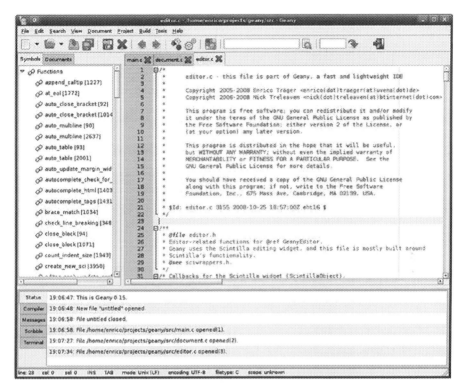

Figure 1-7. *Geany*

PyCharm

PyCharm by JetBrains is another IDE for Python and it's packed with powerful features like a debugger, a code inspection tool, version control, and an integrated unit test runner. It is a cross-platform IDE available for Windows, macOS, and Linux distributions. Its Community Edition is a free download. Visit its home page at **https://www.jetbrains.com/pycharm/** for more information.

The code examples in this book are better suited for execution from the command prompt, due to the nature of the libraries involved. I personally prefer to write the logic and code on paper (Yes! Using a piece of paper!) first and then use a plain-text editor with syntax highlighting. For example,

21

I recommend Notepad++ on Windows, or nano, Leafpad, and gedit on Linux. You can use IDLE3 or Geany for writing and compiling the code.

However, most of the code examples are meant to be executed from the command line.

EXERCISE 1-1

- Visit and explore the Python home page at `www.python.org`.

- Read where Python is deployed successfully at `https://www.python.org/about/success/`.

- Visit and explore the Python documentation page at `https://docs.python.org/3/`.

- Check the version-wise new features of the latest releases of Python at `https://docs.python.org/3/whatsnew/index.html`.

- For practice, write simple programs in Python. For example, you could write programs for a Fibonacci series and factorial calculations using iterative and recursive techniques.

Complete this exercise to understand Python 3's background better.

Conclusion

In this chapter, you learned the background, history, and features of Python. You also studied the important differences between Python 2 and Python 3. You learned how to install and use Python 3 in script and interactive modes. Finally, you looked at a few popular IDEs for Python. In the next chapter, you will get started with the concepts of test automation and look at a simple test automation library for Python, called doctest. You will also briefly look at pydoc.

CHAPTER 2

Getting Started

In the previous chapter, you learned how to set up the Python 3 environment on Linux, macOS, and Windows computers. You also looked at a few popular IDEs for Python. In this chapter, you will get started with concepts of test automation. Then you will explore a light and easy way to learn the test automation framework in Python 3, called doctest.

A Brief Introduction to Software Testing Concepts

The textbook definition of software testing states that it's the process of executing a program or application to find any bugs. Usually, there are multiple stakeholders in the process of software testing. The stakeholders include testers, the management team, consultants, business, customers, and end users. With medium- to large-scale projects, software testing is done to determine if the software behaves as intended under various sets of inputs and conditions.

© Ashwin Pajankar 2022
A. Pajankar, *Python Unit Test Automation*, https://doi.org/10.1007/978-1-4842-7854-3_2

Unit Testing

Unit testing is a software testing method in which individual components of the program, called *units,* are tested independently with all the required dependencies. Unit testing is mostly done by programmers, who write the programs for the units. In smaller projects, it is done informally. In most very large-scale projects, unit testing is part of a formal process of development, with proper documentation and proper schedule/efforts allocated to it.

Test Automation

Test automation is the automated execution and reporting of the outcome of test scenarios and cases. In most large and complex projects, many phases of the testing process are automated. Sometimes the effort of automating tests is so huge that there is a separate project for automation with a separate team dedicated to it, including a separate reporting structure with separate management. There are several areas and phases of testing that can be automated. Various tools like code libraries and third-party APIs are used for unit testing. Sometimes, the code for unit testing is also generated in an automated way. Unit testing is a prime candidate for automation.

The Benefits of Automated Unit Testing

There are many reasons to automate unit tests. Let's consider them one by one.

- Time and effort

   As your codebase grows, the number of modules to be unit tested grows. Manual testing is very time-consuming. To reduce manual testing efforts, you can automate test cases, which then can be automated easily and quickly.

- Accuracy

  Test case execution is a rote and boring activity.
  Humans can make mistakes. However, an automated
  test suite will run and return correct results every time.

- Early bug reporting

  Automating unit test cases gives you the distinct
  advantage of early reporting of bugs and errors. When
  automated test suites are run by the scheduler,
  once the code freezes due to an error, all the logical
  bugs in the code are quickly discovered and reported,
  without much human intervention needed.

- Built-in support for unit testing

  There are many programming languages that provide
  built-in support for writing unit tests by means of
  libraries dedicated to unit testing. Examples include
  Python, Java, and PHP.

Using Docstrings

The focus of this chapter is on getting you started with unit test automation
in Python. Let's get started with the concept of docstrings and their
implementation in Python. Docstrings are going to be immensely useful to
you while learning `doctest`.

A *docstring* is a string literal that's specified in the source code of
a module. It is used to document a specific segment of code. Code
comments are also used for documenting source code. However, there is
a major difference between a docstring and a comment. When the source
code is parsed, the comments are not included in the parsing tree as part
of the code, whereas docstrings are included in the parsed code tree.

The major advantage of this is that the docstrings are available for use at runtime. Using the functionalities specific to the programming language, you can retrieve the docstring specific to a module. Docstrings are always retained through the entire runtime of the module instance.

Example of a Docstring in Python

Let's see how the concept of the docstring is implemented in Python. A Python docstring is a string literal that occurs as the first statement in a module, function, class, or method definition. A docstring becomes the doc special attribute of that object.

Let's take a look at a code example of a Python docstring. From this chapter onward, you will be programming quite a lot. I recommend that you create a directory on your computer and create chapter-specific subdirectories within it. As mentioned earlier, I am using a Linux OS. (My favorite computer, a Raspberry Pi 3 Model B.) I have created a directory called book and a directory called code under that. The code directory has chapter-specific directories containing the code of each chapter. Figure 2-1 shows a graphical representation of the directory structure in the form of a tree diagram.

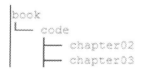

Figure 2-1. *The suggested directory structure for the book*

Create chapter-specific subdirectories under the directory code, as shown in the tree diagram in Figure 2-1. We use the directory chapter02 for this chapter, chapter03 for the next chapter, and so on. Navigate to the chapter02 directory and save the following code (see Listing 2-1) as test_module01.py in that directory.

Listing 2-1. test_module01.py

```
"""
This is test_module01.
This is example of multiline docstring. """

class TestClass01:
    """This is TestClass01."""

  def test_case01(self):
    """This is test_case01()."""

def test_function01():
    """This is  test_function01()."""
```

In Listing 2-1, there is a test file called test_module01.py, which includes TestClass01 and test_function01(). TestClass01 has a method called test_ case01(). There is a docstring for all code units here. The first docstring is a multiline docstring. The rest are examples of single-line docstrings.

Let's see how the docstrings work using the code in Listing 2-1 and an interactive Python session.

Navigate to the chapter02 directory and type python3 to invoke Python 3 in interpreter mode.

```
pi@raspberrypi:~/book/code/chapter02 $ pwd
/home/pi/book/code/chapter02
pi@raspberrypi:~/book/code/chapter02 $
python3 Python 3.4.2 (default, Oct 19 2014, 13:31:11)
[GCC 4.9.1] on linux
Type "help", "copyright", "credits" or "license" for more
information.
>>>
```

Import the test module you just created with the following statement:

```
>>> import test_module01
```

You can use the help() function to see the docstrings of the module and its members, as follows.

```
>>> help(test_module01)
```

The output is as follows:

```
Help on module test_module01:

NAME
    test_module01

DESCRIPTION
    This is test_module01.
    This is example of multiline docstring.

CLASSES
    builtins.object
      TestClass01

class TestClass01(builtins.object)
 |   This is TestClass01.
 |
 |   Methods defined here:
 |
 |   test_case01(self)
 |       This is test_case01().
 |
 |_____
```

```
| Data descriptors defined here:
|
|  __dict
|       dictionary for instance variables (if defined)
|
|  __weakref
|        list of weak references to the object (if defined)
FUNCTIONS
    test_function01()
        This is test_function01().
FILE
      /home/pi/book/code/chapter02/test_module01.py
```

You can see the docstring of the individual members using help(). Run the following statements and see the output for yourself.

```
>>> help(test_module01.TestClass01)
>>> help(test_module01.TestClass01.test_case01)
>>> help(test_module01.test_function01)
```

As mentioned earlier, a docstring becomes the doc special attribute of that object. You can also use the print() function to see the docstring of a module and its members. The following interactive Python session demonstrates that.

```
>>> import test_module01
>>> print(test_module01._doc_)

This is test_module01.
This is example of multiline docstring.

>>> print(test_module01.TestClass01._doc_)
This is TestClass01.
```

```
>>> print(test_module01.TestClass01.test_case01._doc_)
This is test_case01().
>>> print(test_module01.test_function01._doc_)
This is test_function01().
>>>
```

You can find detailed information about the Python docstring on the following PEP pages.

```
https://www.python.org/dev/peps/pep-0256
https://www.python.org/dev/peps/pep-0257
https://www.python.org/dev/peps/pep-0258
```

In the next section, you learn to use docstrings to write simple test cases and execute them with doctest.

A Brief Introduction to doctest

doctest is the lightweight unit-testing framework in Python that uses docstrings to test automation. doctest is packaged with the Python interpreter, so you do not have to install anything separately to use it. It is part of Python's standard library and adheres to Python's "batteries-included" philosophy.

Note   If you're interested, you can read Python's batteries-included philosophy on the PEP 206 page (see `https://www.python.org/dev/peps/pep-0206`).

The code in Listing 2-2 is a simple example of a test module with two functions and two tests for each function.

Listing 2-2. test_module02.py

```
"""
Sample doctest test module... test_module02
"""

def mul(a, b):
    """
>>> mul(2, 3)
    6
>>> mul('a', 2)
    'aa'
    """

    return a * b

def add(a, b):
    """
>>> add(2, 3)
    5
>>> add('a', 'b')
    'ab'
    """

    return a + b
```

In Listing 2-2, the test cases are mentioned as docstrings for the
modules and there is nothing specifically calling the doctest in the code
itself. When the program is executed as a Python 3 program using the
python3 test command, _module02.py does not produce any output at
the command line. In order to see doctest in action, you have to run it
using the following command at the command prompt:

```
python3 -m doctest -v test_module02.py
```

The output will be as follows:

```
Trying:
     add(2, 3)
Expecting:
     5
ok
Trying:
     add('a', 'b')
Expecting:
     'ab'
ok
Trying:
     mul(2, 3)
Expecting:
     6
ok
Trying:
     mul('a', 2)
Expecting:
     'aa'
ok
1.  items had no tests:
    test_module02
2.  items passed all tests:
   2 tests in test_module02.add
   2 tests in test_module02.mul
4 tests in 3 items.
4 passed and 0 failed.
Test passed.
```

Let's take a look at how doctest works. By comparing the code—specifically the commands for execution and output—you can figure out quite a few things. doctest works by parsing docstrings. Whenever doctest finds an interactive Python prompt in the doctest documentation of a module, it treats its output as the expected output. Then it runs the module and its members by referring to the docstrings. It compares the actual output against the output specified in the docstrings. Then it marks the test pass or fail. You have to use -m doctest while executing the module to let the interpreter know that you need to use the doctest module to execute the code.

The command-line argument -v stands for *verbose* mode. You must use it because, without it, the test will not produce any output unless it fails. Using verbose produces an execution log irrespective of whether the test passes or fails.

Failing Tests

In Listing 2-2, all the tests passed with no hassles. Now, let's see how a test fails. In Listing 2-2, replace + on the last line of the code with an * (asterisk) and run the test again with the same command. You will get the following output:

```
Trying:
    add(2, 3)
Expecting:
    5
**************************************************************
File "/home/pi/book/code/chapter02/test_module02.py", line 19,
in test_module02.add
Failed example:
    add(2, 3)
Expected:
    5
Got:
    6
```

```
Trying:
    add('a', 'b')
Expecting:
    'ab'
**********************************************************
File "/home/pi/book/code/chapter02/test_module02.py", line 21,
in test_module02.add
Failed example:
    add('a', 'b')
Exception raised:
    Traceback (most recent call last):
      File "/usr/lib/python3.4/doctest.py", line 1324, in_run
        compileflags, 1), test.globs)
      File "<doctest test_module02.add[1]>", line 1,
      in <module>
        add('a', 'b')
      File "/home/pi/book/code/chapter02/test_module02.py",
      line 24, in add
        return a * b
TypeError: can't multiply sequence by non-int of type 'str'
Trying:
    mul(2, 3)
Expecting:
    6
ok
Trying:
    mul('a', 2)
Expecting:
    'aa'
```

```
ok
1 items had no tests:
    test_module02
1 items passed all tests:
    2 tests in test_module02.mul
**************************************************************
1 items had failures:
    2 of   2 in test_module02.add
4 tests in 3 items.
2 passed and 2 failed.
***Test Failed*** 2 failures.
```

You can clearly see two failures in the execution log. The tests usually fail due to one or more of the following reasons:

- Faulty logic in the code

- Faulty input into the code

- Faulty test case

In this case, there are two failures in the test. The first one is due to faulty logic. The second failure is due to faulty logic in the code and the wrong type of input given to the function to be tested.

Correct the code by replacing the * in the last line with +. Then change the line that has 'aa' to aa and run the test again. This will demonstrate the third cause of test failure (a faulty test case).

Separate Test File

You can also write your tests in a separate test file and run them separately from the code to be tested. This helps maintain the test modules/code separately from the development code. Create a file called test_module03.txt in the same directory and add the code shown in Listing 2-3 to it.

Listing 2-3. test_module03.txt

```
>>> from test_module02 import *
>>> mul(2, 3)
6
>>> mul('a', 2)
'aa'
>>> add(2, 3)
5
>>> add('a', 'b')
'ab'
```

You can run this test in the usual way, by running the following command in the command prompt:

```
python3 -m doctest -v test_module03.txt
```

The output will be as follows:

```
Trying:
    from test_module02 import *
Expecting nothing
ok
Trying:
    mul(2, 3)
Expecting:
    6
ok
Trying:
    mul('a', 2)
Expecting:
    'aa'
ok
```

```
Trying:
     add(2, 3)
Expecting:
     5
ok
Trying:
     add('a', 'b')
Expecting:
     'ab'
ok
1 items passed all tests:
5 tests in test_module03.txt
5 tests in 1 items.
5 passed and 0 failed.
Test passed.
```

Advantages and Disadvantages of doctest

As you have learned, doctest is a very simple and intuitive framework for novice-level testing in Python. It does not require any installation and you can quickly get started with it without needing to know any API. It is mostly used for the following purposes:

- To verify if the code documentation is up to date and the interactive examples in the docstring still work after making changes to the code.

- To perform module-wise basic regression testing.

- To write illustrative tutorials and documentation that doubles as a test case for the package and module.

However, doctest has its own set of limitations. It does not have true API for testing.

doctest tests also tend to be static in nature and cannot be parameterized.

You are advised to visit the doctest documentation page at https://docs.python.org/3/library/doctest.html for detailed usage and more examples.

Pydoc

Just like doctest, there is another useful utility to view the documentation of a module. It comes with Python. It is known as Pydoc. On Linux, run the following command:

```
pydoc unittest
```

It will show the documentation of the unittest library. If you have created the documentation for your own custom module with docstrings, you can view it with the following command:

```
pydoc test_module01
```

This command displays the documentation on the terminal. You can save all this information in HTML files as follows:

```
pydoc -w unittest
pydoc -w test_module01
```

These commands will create unittest.html and test_module01.html documents in the directory where the commands are run. You can then open these files with a web browser of your choice.

On Windows, the commands can be run as follows:

```
python -m pydoc unittest
python -m pydoc -w unittest
```

Conclusion

In this chapter, you learned the basics of software testing. You explored a light testing framework, called doctest. It's a good module for simple projects for novice Python users. However, due to its lack of advanced features like testrunner, test discovery, and test fixtures, doctest is not used in large projects. The next chapter discusses a built-in xUnit style test automation framework for Python, called unittest.

CHAPTER 3

unittest

The last chapter discussed the concepts of test automation. You learned about docstring and doctest and their use in writing simple, static, yet elegant test cases for Python 3 programs. However, due to lack of features, like API, configurable tests, and test fixtures, doctest enjoys very limited popularity. You need to explore a powerful API library for automating complex real-life projects and learning Python's built-in unittest module is your first step toward it.

This is a detailed and long chapter. You will learn many new concepts like test fixtures, automated test discovery, organizing your codebase, and so on, in this chapter. You will use these concepts throughout the book and see their implementation in more advanced test automation libraries in Python. So, I recommend that you follow every topic in this chapter very carefully.

unittest came to life as a third-party module called PyUnit. PyUnit was the Python port for JUnit. JUnit is Java's xUnit-style unit test automation framework.

PyUnit became part of the Python Standard library from version 2.5 onward. It was rechristened unittest. unittest is the *batteries-included* test automation library of Python, which means you do not have to install an additional library or tool in order to start using it. Anyone who is familiar with xUnit-style libraries in other programming languages (such as JUnit for Java, PHPUnit for PHP, CPPUnit for C++, etc.) will find it very easy to learn and use unittest.

© Ashwin Pajankar 2022
A. Pajankar, *Python Unit Test Automation*, https://doi.org/10.1007/978-1-4842-7854-3_3

Introduction to xUnit

Let's take a look at the xUnit philosophy in brief. xUnit is the collective name for several unit-testing frameworks for various languages. All the xUnit-style unit testing frameworks more or less derive their functionality, structure, and coding style from Smalltalk's unit testing framework, called SUnit. Kent Beck designed and wrote SUnit. After it gained popularity, it was ported to Java as JUnit by Kent Beck and Erich Gamma. Eventually, it was ported to almost every programming language. Now most programming languages come prepackaged with at least one xUnit-style test automation library. Also, many programming languages like Python and Java have more than one xUnit-style framework. Java has TestNG in addition to JUnit. Python has nose, pytest, and Nose2 apart from unittest.

All the xUnit-style test automation libraries follow a common architecture. The following are the major components of the architecture:

- *Test case class*: This is the base class of all the test classes in the test modules. All the test classes are derived from here.

- *Test fixtures*: These are functions or methods that run before and after blocks of test code execute.

- *Assertions*: These functions or methods are used to check the behavior of the component being tested. Most of the xUnit-style frameworks are packed with powerful assertion methods.

- *Test suite*: This is a collection or group of related tests that can be executed or scheduled to be executed together.

- *Test runner*: This is a program or block of code that runs the test suite.

- *Test result formatter*: This formats the test results to produce the output of test execution in various human readable formats like plaintext, HTML, and XML.

The implementation details of these components of xUnit differ slightly across unit testing frameworks. Interestingly, this enables programmers to choose the framework based on the needs of their projects and their comfort.

If you are a seasoned programmer who has experience with any of these frameworks, you will quickly be able to translate your knowledge to Python code. If you do not have prior experience with any of the xUnit-style frameworks, then after reading the book, executing all the examples in the book and solving all the exercises, you can get started with any of the xUnit frameworks on your own without much hand-holding.

Using unittest

This section starts with unittest. It begins with the most fundamental concept of a test class.

For this chapter, create a directory called chapter03 in the code directory. In chapter03, create another directory called test (you will learn later in the chapter why you need that additional directory). Save the code in Listing 3-1 as test_module01.py.

Listing 3-1. test_module01.py

```python
import unittest
class TestClass01(unittest.TestCase):
    def test_case01(self):
        my_str = "ASHWIN"
        my_int = 999
        self.assertTrue(isinstance(my_str, str))
        self.assertTrue(isinstance(my_int, int))
```

```
    def test_case02(self):
        my_pi = 3.14
        self.assertFalse(isinstance(my_pi, int))

if __name__ == '__main__':
    unittest.main()
```

In the code in Listing 3-1, the import unittest statement imports the unittest module. TestClass01 is the test class. It is subclassed from the TestCase class in the unittest module. The test_case01() and test_case02() class methods are test methods, as their names start with test_ (You will learn about the guidelines and naming conventions for writing tests later in this chapter.) The assertTrue() and assertFalse() methods are assertion methods that check if the argument passed to them is True or False, respectively. If the argument meets the assert condition, the test case passes; otherwise, it fails. unittest.main() is the test runner. You will explore more assert methods in detail later.

Navigate to the test directory as follows:

```
cd ~/book/code/chapter03/test
```

Run the following command:

```
python3 test_module01.py
```

It yields the following output:

```
----------------------------------------------------------
Ran 2 tests in 0.002s
OK
```

It says OK, as both tests passed. This is one of the ways you can write and execute tests.

The test execution did not display much information. That's because verbosity is disabled by default. You can run the tests in verbose mode using the -v command-line option. Run the following command at the command prompt:

```
python3 test_module01.py -v
```

The verbose output is as follows:

```
test_case01 ( main .TestClass01) ... ok
test_case02 ( main .TestClass01) ... ok
----------------------------------------------------------
Ran 2 tests in 0.004s
OK
```

Certainly, verbose execution mode provides more insight about test execution. You will be using this mode very frequently throughout the book for running tests and gathering the log for test executions.

Order of Execution of the Test Methods

Now, you will see the order in which the test methods are executed. Check out the code in Listing 3-2.

Listing 3-2. test_module02.py

```
import unittest
import inspect
class TestClass02(unittest.TestCase):
    def test_case02(self):
        print("\nRunning Test Method : " + inspect.
        stack()[0][3])
```

```
    def test_case01(self):
        print("\nRunning Test Method : " + inspect.
        stack()[0][3])

if  name   == ' main ':
    unittest.main(verbosity=2)
```

In the code in Listing 3-2, the `inspect.stack()[0][3]` method prints the name of the current test method. It's useful for debugging when you want to know the order that the methods are executed in the test class. The output of the code in Listing 3-2 is as follows:

```
test_case01 ( main .TestClass02) ...
Running Test Method : test_case01
ok
test_case02 ( main .TestClass02) ...
Running Test Method : test_case02
ok
-----------------------------------------------------------
Ran 2 tests in 0.090s
OK
```

Note that the test methods ran in alphabetical order, irrespective of the order of the test methods in the code.

Verbosity Control

In earlier examples, you controlled the verbosity of test execution through the command while invoking the Python test script in the OS console. Now, you will learn how to control verbose mode from the code itself. The code in Listing 3-3 shows an example.

Listing 3-3. test_module03.py

```python
import unittest
import inspect

def add(x, y):
    print("We're in custom made function : " + inspect.
    stack()[0][3])
    return(x + y)
class TestClass03(unittest.TestCase):
    def test_case01(self):
        print("\nRunning Test Method : " + inspect.
        stack()[0][3])
        self.assertEqual(add(2, 3), 5)

    def test_case02(self):
        print("\nRunning Test Method : " + inspect.
        stack()[0][3])
        my_var = 3.14
        self.assertTrue(isinstance(my_var, float))

    def test_case03(self):
        print("\nRunning Test Method : " + inspect.
        stack()[0][3])
        self.assertEqual(add(2, 2), 5)

    def test_case04(self):
        print("\nRunning Test Method : " + inspect.
        stack()[0][3])
        my_var = 3.14
        self.assertTrue(isinstance(my_var, int))

if   name   == ' main ':
    unittest.main(verbosity=2)
```

In Listing 3-3, you are testing a custom function called add() with the assertEqual() method. assertEqual() takes two arguments and determines if both arguments are equal. If both arguments are equal, the test case passes; otherwise, it fails. There is also a function called add() in the same test module that's not a member of the test class. With test_case01() and test_case03(), you are testing the correctness of the function.

The code also sets verbosity to the value 2 in the unittest.main() statement.

Run the code in Listing 3-3 with the following command:

```
python3 test_module03.py
```

The output is as follows:

```
test_case01 ( main .TestClass03) ...
Running Test Method : test_case01
We're in custom made function : add
ok
test_case02 ( main .TestClass03) ...
Running Test Method : test_case02
ok
test_case03 ( main .TestClass03) ...
Running Test Method : test_case03
We're in custom made function : add
FAIL
test_case04 ( main .TestClass03) ...
Running Test Method : test_case04
FAIL

===========================================================
FAIL: test_case03 ( main .TestClass03)
-----------------------------------------------------------
```

```
Traceback (most recent call last):
   File "test_module03.py", line 23, in test_case03
      self.assertEqual(add(2, 2), 5)
AssertionError: 4 != 5


==============================================================
FAIL: test_case04 ( main .TestClass03)
--------------------------------------------------------------
Traceback (most recent call last):
   File "test_module03.py", line 28, in test_case04
      self.assertTrue(isinstance(my_var, int))
AssertionError: False is not true
--------------------------------------------------------------
Ran 4 tests in 0.112s
FAILED (failures=2)
```

The test_case03() and test_case04() test cases failed because the assert conditions failed. You now have more information related to the test case failure, since verbosity was enabled in the code.

Multiple Test Classes Within the Same Test File/Module

Until now, the examples included a single test class in a single test file. A .py file that contains the test class is also called a *test module*. Listing 3-4 shows an example of a test module that has multiple test classes.

Listing 3-4. test_module04.py

```
import unittest
import inspect
class TestClass04(unittest.TestCase):
    def test_case01(self):
        print("\nClassname : " + self. class . name )
        print("Running Test Method : " + inspect.stack()[0][3])
```

51

```
class TestClass05(unittest.TestCase):
    def test_case01(self):
        print("\nClassname : " + self. class . name )
        print("Running Test Method : " + inspect.stack()[0][3])

if  name   == ' main ':
    unittest.main(verbosity=2)
```

The following is the output after running the code in Listing 3-4:

```
test_case01 ( main .TestClass04) ...
Classname : TestClass04
Running Test Method : test_case01
ok
test_case01 ( main .TestClass05) ...
Classname : TestClass05
Running Test Method : test_case01
ok
-----------------------------------------------------------
Ran 2 tests in 0.080s
OK
```

All the test classes are executed one by one in alphabetical order.

Test Fixtures

To put it simply, *test fixtures* are the set of steps performed before and after the tests.

In unittest, these are implemented as methods of the TestCase class and can be overridden for your purposes. An example of custom test fixtures in unittest is shown in Listing 3-5.

Listing 3-5. test_module05.py

```python
import unittest

def setUpModule():
    """called once, before anything else in this module"""
    print("In setUpModule()...")

def tearDownModule():
    """called once, after everything else in this module"""
    print("In tearDownModule()...")
class TestClass06(unittest.TestCase):
    @classmethod
    def setUpClass(cls):
        """called once, before any test"""
        print("In setUpClass()...")

    @classmethod
    def tearDownClass(cls):
        """called once, after all tests, if setUpClass
            successful"""
        print("In tearDownClass()...")

    def setUp(self):
        """called multiple times, before every test method"""
        print("\nIn setUp()...")

    def tearDown(self):
        """called multiple times, after every test method"""
        print("In tearDown()...")
```

```
    def test_case01(self):
        self.assertTrue("PYTHON".isupper())
        print("In test_case01()")

    def test_case02(self):
        self.assertFalse("python".isupper())
        print("In test_case02()")

if  name   == ' main ':
    unittest.main()
```

In the code in Listing 3-5, the setUpModule() and tearDownModule() methods are the module-level fixtures. setUpModule() is executed before any method in the test module. tearDownModule() is executed after all methods in the test module. setUpClass() and tearDownClass() are class-level fixtures. setUpClass() is executed before any method in the test class. tearDownClass() is executed after all methods in the test class.

These methods are used with the @classmethod decorator, as shown in the code in Listing 3-5. The @classmethod decorator must have a reference to a class object as the first parameter. setUp() and tearDown() are method-level fixtures. setUp() and tearDown() methods are executed before and after every test method in the test class. Run the code in Listing 3-5 as follows:

```
python3 test_module05.py -v
```

The following is the output of the code:

```
In setUpModule()...
In setUpClass()...
test_case01 ( main .TestClass06) ...
In setUp()...
In test_case01()
In tearDown()...
```

```
ok
test_case02 ( main .TestClass06) ... In
setUp()...
In test_case02()
In tearDown()...
ok
In tearDownClass()...
In tearDownModule()...
-----------------------------------------------------------
Ran 2 tests in 0.004s
OK
```

The test fixtures and their implementation are a key feature of any test automation library. This is a major advantage over the static testing offered by doctest.

Running Without unittest.main( )

Up until now, you have run the test modules with unittest.main(). Now you will see how to run the test module without unittest.main(). Consider the code in Listing 3-6, for example.

Listing 3-6. test_module06.py

```
import unittest
class TestClass07(unittest.TestCase):
    def test_case01(self):
        self.assertTrue("PYTHON".isupper())
        print("\nIn test_case01()")
```

If you try to run it the usual way, with python3 test_module06.py, you do not get output in the console, as it does not have the if name =='main ' and unittest. main() statements in it. Even running in verbose mode with python3 test_module06.py -v does not yield any output in the console.

The only way to run this module is to use the Python interpreter with the -m unittest option and the module name, as follows:

```
python -m unittest test_module06
```

The output is as follows:

```
In test_case01()
.
----------------------------------------------------------
Ran 1 test in 0.002s
OK
```

Note that you do not need to have .py after the module name as you did earlier. You can also enable verbosity with the -v options, as follows:

```
python -m unittest test_module06 -v
```

The verbose output is as follows:

```
test_case01 (test_module06.TestClass07) ...
In test_case01()
ok
----------------------------------------------------------
Ran 1 test in 0.002s

OK
```

You will use this same method throughout the chapter to run test modules. In later sections of this chapter, you will learn more about this method. For now, run all the previous code examples with this method of execution as an exercise.

Controlling the Granularity of Test Execution

You learned how to run a test module using the -m unittest option. You can also run individual test classes and test cases using this option.

Consider the earlier example of test_module04.py again, shown in Listing 3-7.

Listing 3-7. test_module04.py

```
import unittest
import inspect

class TestClass04(unittest.TestCase):

    def test_case01(self):
        print("\nClassname : " + self. class . name )
        print("Running Test Method : " + inspect.stack()[0][3])
class TestClass05(unittest.TestCase):
    def test_case01(self):
        print("\nClassname : " + self. class . name )
        print("Running Test Method : " + inspect.stack()[0][3])

if  name   == ' main ':
    unittest.main(verbosity=2)
```

You can run the entire test module with the following command:

```
python3 -m unittest -v test_module04
```

The output is as follows:

```
test_case01 (test_module04.TestClass04) ...
Classname : TestClass04
Running Test Method : test_case01
ok
test_case01 (test_module04.TestClass05) ...
```

```
Classname : TestClass05
Running Test Method : test_case01
ok
-----------------------------------------------------------
Ran 2 tests in 0.090s OK
```

You can run a single test class with the following command:

```
python3 -m unittest -v test_module04.TestClass04
```

The output is as follows:

```
test_case01 (test_module04.TestClass04) ...
Classname : TestClass04
Running Test Method : test_case01
ok
-----------------------------------------------------------
Ran 1 test in 0.077s
OK
```

You can also run a single test case with the following command:

```
python3 -m unittest -v test_module04.TestClass05.test_case01
```

The output is as follows:

```
test_case01 (test_module04.TestClass05) ...
Classname : TestClass05
Running Test Method : test_case01
ok
-----------------------------------------------------------
Ran 1 test in 0.077s
OK
```

This way, you can control the granularity of the test execution.

Listing All the Command-Line Options and Help

You can list all the command-line options of unittest using the -h command-line option. Run the following command:

```
python3 -m unittest -h
```

The following is the output:

```
usage: python3 -m unittest [-h] [-v] [-q] [-f] [-c] [-b] [tests
[tests ...]] positional arguments:
tests    a list of any number of test modules, classes and test
methods.

optional arguments:
-h, --help   show this help message and exit
-v, --verbose   Verbose output
-q, --quiet   Quiet output
-f, --failfast Stop on first fail or error
-c, --catch   Catch ctrl-C and display results so far
-b, --buffer   Buffer stdout and stderr during tests

Examples:
python3 -m unittest test_module   - run tests from test_module
python3 -m unittest module.TestClass   - run tests from module.
TestClass
python3 -m unittest module.Class.test_method - run specified
test method

usage: python3 -m unittest discover [-h] [-v] [-q] [-f] [-c]
[-b] [-s START] [-p PATTERN] [-t TOP]

optional arguments:
-h, --help      show this help message and exit
-v, --verbose      Verbose output
-q, --quiet      Quiet output
```

```
-f, --failfast     Stop on first fail or error
-c, --catch        Catch ctrl-C and display results so far
-b, --buffer       Buffer stdout and stderr during tests
-s START, --start-directory START
                   Directory to start discovery ('.' default)
-p PATTERN, --pattern PATTERN
                   Pattern to match tests ('test*.py' default)
-t TOP, --top-level-directory TOP
                   Top level directory of project (defaults to
                   start directory)
```

For test discovery all test modules must be importable from the top level directory of the project.

This way you get a detailed summary of the various command-line options available with unittest.

Important Command-Line Options

Let's take a look at the important command-line options in unittest. Take a look at the code in Listing 3-8 for example.

Listing 3-8. test_module07.py

```python
import unittest
class TestClass08(unittest.TestCase): def test_case01(self):
            self.assertTrue("PYTHON".isupper())
            print("\nIn test_case1()")

        def test_case02(self):
            self.assertTrue("Python".isupper())
            print("\nIn test_case2()")

        def test_case03(self):
            self.assertTrue(True) print("\nIn test_case3()")
```

You already know that -v stands for verbose mode. The following is the output in verbose mode:

```
test_case01 (test_module07.TestClass08) ...
In test_case1()
ok
test_case02 (test_module07.TestClass08) ... FAIL
test_case03 (test_module07.TestClass08) ...
In test_case3()
ok


================================================
FAIL: test_case02 (test_module07.TestClass08)
----------------------------------------------------------
Traceback (most recent call last):
  File "/home/pi/book/code/chapter03/test/test_module07.py",
  line 11, in test_case02
   self.assertTrue("Python".isupper())
AssertionError: False is not true
----------------------------------------------------------
Ran 3 tests in 0.012s
FAILED (failures=1)
```

The -q option stands for *quiet* mode. Run the following command to demonstrate quiet mode:

```
python3 -m unittest -q test_module07
```

The output is as follows:

```
In test_case1()
In test_case3()
```

```
==================================================
FAIL: test_case02 (test_module07.TestClass08)
--------------------------------------------------------
Traceback (most recent call last):
   File "/home/pi/book/code/chapter03/test/test_module07.py",
   line 11, in test_case02
   self.assertTrue("Python".isupper())
AssertionError: False is not true
--------------------------------------------------------

Ran 3 tests in 0.005s
FAILED (failures=1)
```

The -f option stands for *failsafe*. It forcefully stops execution as soon as the first test case fails. Run the following command to initiate failsafe mode:

```
python3 -m unittest -f test_module07
```

The following is the output in failsafe mode:

```
In test_case1()
.F
============================================================
FAIL: test_case02 (test_module07.TestClass08)
--------------------------------------------------------
Traceback (most recent call last):
   File "/home/pi/book/code/chapter03/test/test_module07.py",
   line 11, in test_case02
    self.assertTrue("Python".isupper())
AssertionError: False is not true
--------------------------------------------------------

Ran 2 tests in 0.004s
FAILED (failures=1)
```

You can also use more than one option. For example, you can combine verbose with failsafe using the following command:

```
python3 -m unittest -fv test_module07
```

The output is as follows:

```
test_case01 (test_module07.TestClass08) ...
In test_case1()
ok
test_case02 (test_module07.TestClass08) ... FAIL

============================================================
FAIL: test_case02 (test_module07.TestClass08)
------------------------------------------------------------
Traceback (most recent call last):
    File "/home/pi/book/code/chapter03/test/test_module07.py",
    line 11, in test_case02
    self.assertTrue("Python".isupper())
AssertionError: False is not true
------------------------------------------------------------
Ran 2 tests in 0.005s
FAILED (failures=1)
```

As an exercise, try to use different combinations of command-line options.

Creating a Test Package

Up until now, you have created and executed test modules individually. However, you can use Python's built-in packaging feature to create a package of tests. This is standard practice in complex projects with large codebases.

Figure 3-1 shows a snapshot of the current `test` directory where you are saving your test modules.

```
pi@raspberrypi:~/book/code/chapter03/test $ tree
.
├── test_module01.py
├── test_module02.py
├── test_module03.py
├── test_module04.py
├── test_module05.py
├── test_module06.py
└── test_module07.py
```

***Figure 3-1.** Snapshot of the test subdirectory in the chapter03 directory*

Now, let's create a package of test modules. Create an `init.py` file in the `test` directory. Add the code in Listing 3-9 to the `init.py` file.

***Listing 3-9.** init.py*

```
all = ["test_module01", "test_module02", "test_module03",
"test_module04", "test_module05", "test_module06",
"test_module07"]
```

Congratulations! You just created a test package. `test` is the name of the testing package and all modules mentioned in `init.py` belong to this package. If you need to add a new testing module to the `test` package, you need to create a new test module file in the `test` directory and then add the name of that module to the `init.py` file.

Now you can run the test modules from the parent directory of `test` (`chapter03`) in the following way. Move to the `chapter03` directory using the following command:

```
cd /home/pi/book/code/chapter03
```

Note that the path might be different in your case, depending on where you created the book directory.

Run the test module with the following command:

```
python3 -m unittest -v test.test_module04
```

The following is the output:

```
test_case01 (test.test_module04.TestClass04) ...
Classname : TestClass04
Running Test Method : test_case01
ok
test_case01 (test.test_module04.TestClass05) ...
Classname : TestClass05
Running Test Method : test_case01
ok
------------------------------------------------------------
Ran 2 tests in 0.090s
OK
```

Run a test class in the test module with the following command:

```
python3 -m unittest -v test.test_module04.TestClass04
```

The output is as follows:

```
test_case01 (test.test_module04.TestClass04) ...
Classname : TestClass04
Running Test Method : test_case01
ok
------------------------------------------------------------
Ran 1 test in 0.078s
OK
```

Run a test case from a test module as follows:

```
python3 -m unittest -v test.test_module04.TestClass04.
test_case01
```

The output is as follows:

```
test_case01 (test.test_module04.TestClass04) ...
Classname : TestClass04
Running Test Method : test_case01
ok
----------------------------------------------------------
Ran 1 test in 0.079s
OK
```

Organizing the Code

Let's look at ways you can organize the test code and the dev code. You're now moving toward real-life project scenarios for using unittest. Up until now, the tests (the testing code) and the code to be tested (the development code) were in the same module. Usually in real-life projects, the development code and the test code are kept in different files.

Placing the Development and Test Code in a Single Directory

Here, you will organize the dev and test code into a single directory. In the test directory, create a module called test_me.py and add the code in Listing 3-10 to it.

Listing 3-10. test_me.py

```
def add(x, y):
    return(x + y)
```

```
def mul(x, y):
    return(x * y)

def sub(x, y):
    return(x - y)

def div(x, y):
    return(x / y)
```

Now, since test_me.py is in the test directory, it can directly be imported into another module in the same directory using the import test_me statement. The test module in Listing 3-11 imports test_me.py to test its functionality.

Listing 3-11. test_module08.py

```
import unittest
import test_me
class TestClass09(unittest.TestCase):
    def test_case01(self):
        self.assertEqual(test_me.add(2, 3), 5)
        print("\nIn test_case01()")

    def test_case02(self):
        self.assertEqual(test_me.mul(2, 3), 6)
        print("\nIn test_case02()")
```

Run the test module with the following command:

```
python3 -m unittest -v test_module08
```

The output is as follows:

```
test_case01 (test_module08.TestClass09) ...
In test_case01()
ok
```

```
test_case02 (test_module08.TestClass09) ...
In test_case02()
ok
----------------------------------------------------------
Ran 2 tests in 0.004s OK
```

This way, you can organize the development code and the testing code in the same directory, in different files.

Placing the Development and Test Code in Separate Directories

Many coding standards recommend that the development code and the testing code files be organized in separate directories. Let's do that now.

Navigate to the chapter03 directory:

```
cd /home/pi/book/code/chapter03
```

Create a new directory called mypackage in the chapter03 directory:

```
mkdir mypackage
```

Navigate to the mypackage directory:

```
cd mypackage
```

Save the code in Listing 3-12 as mymathlib.py in the mypackage directory.

Listing 3-12. mymathlib.py

```
class mymathlib:
    def init (self):
        """Constructor for this class..."""
        print("Creating object : " + self. class . name )
```

```
def add(self, x, y):
    return(x + y)

def mul(self, x, y):
    return(x * y)

def mul(self, x, y):
    return(x - y)

def   del (self):
    """Destructor for this class..."""
    print("Destroying object : " + self. class . name )
```

Save the code in Listing 3-13 as mymathsimple.py in the mypackage directory.

Listing 3-13. mymathsimple.py

```
def add(x, y):
    return(x + y)

def mul(x, y):
    return(x * y)

def sub(x, y):
    return(x - y)

def div(x, y):
    return(x / y)
```

These modules you just created are the development modules. Finally, to create a package of development modules, create the init.py file with the code shown in Listing 3-14.

Listing 3-14. init.py

```
all = ["mymathlib", "mymathsimple"]
```

This will create a Python package for the development code. Navigate back to the chapter03 directory. The structure of the chapter03 directory should now look like Figure 3-2.

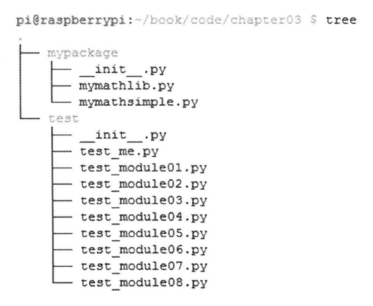

Figure 3-2. *Snapshot of the chapter03 directory*

mypackage is the development code package and test is the testing code package.

You now need to create a test module to test the development code in mypackage. Create a new test module called test_module09.py in the test directory and add the code shown in Listing 3-15.

Listing 3-15. test_module09.py

```python
from mypackage.mymathlib import *
import unittest

math_obj = 0

def setUpModule():
    """"called once, before anything else in the module"""
    print("In setUpModule()...")
    global math_obj
    math_obj = mymathlib()

def tearDownModule():
    """"called once, after everything else in the module"""
    print("In tearDownModule()...")
    global math_obj
    del math_obj

class TestClass10(unittest.TestCase):

    @classmethod
    def setUpClass(cls):
        """"called only once, before any test in the class"""
        print("In setUpClass()...")

    def setUp(self):
        """"called once before every test method"""
        print("\nIn setUp()...")

    def test_case01(self):
        print("In test_case01()")
        self.assertEqual(math_obj.add(2, 5), 7)
```

```
def test_case02(self):
   print("In test_case02()")

def tearDown(self):
   """called once after every test method"""
   print("In tearDown()...")

@classmethod
def tearDownClass(cls):
   """called once, after all the tests in the class"""
   print("In tearDownClass()...")
```

Add test_module09 to init.py in the test directory to make it part of the test package.

Run the code from the test directory using the following command:

```
python3 -m unittest -v test_module09
```

It will throw an error as follows:

```
from mypackage.mymathlib import *
ImportError: No module named 'mypackage'
```

That's because the mypackage module is not visible from the test directory. It lives not in the test directory, but in the chapter03 directory. This module cannot be executed from the test directory. You must execute this module as a part of the test package. You can do this from the chapter03 directory. The mypackage module is visible in this directory as mypackage, which is a subdirectory of chapter03.

Navigate to the chapter03 directory and run this module as follows:

```
python3 -m unittest -v test.test_module09
```

Here is the output of the execution:

```
In setUpModule()...
Creating object : mymathlib
```

```
In setUpClass()...
test_case01 (test.test_module09.TestClass10) ...
In setUp()...
In test_case01()
In tearDown()...
ok
test_case02 (test.test_module09.TestClass10) ...
In setUp()...
In test_case02()
In tearDown()...
ok
In tearDownClass()...
In tearDownModule()...
Destroying object : mymathlib
----------------------------------------------------------
Ran 2 tests in 0.004s
OK
```

That's how you organize the development and testing code files in separate directories. It is standard practice to separate these code files.

Test Discovery

Test discovery is the process of discovering and executing all tests in the project directory and all its subdirectories. The test discovery process is automated in unittest and can be invoked using the discover subcommand. It can be invoked with the following command:

```
python3 -m unittest discover
```

Here is the partial output of this command when it runs in the chapter03 directory:

```
..
Running Test Method : test_case01
.
Running Test Method : test_case02
.
Running Test Method : test_case01
We're in custom made function : add
.
Running Test Method : test_case02
.
Running Test Method : test_case03
We're in custom made function : add
F
Running Test Method : test_case04
F
Classname : TestClass04
Running Test Method : test_case01
```

You can also invoke it using verbose mode with the following command:

```
python3 -m unittest discover -v
```

Here is partial output of this command:

```
test_case01 (test.test_module01.TestClass01) ... ok
test_case02 (test.test_module01.TestClass01) ... ok
test_case01 (test.test_module02.TestClass02) ...
Running Test Method : test_case01
ok
test_case02 (test.test_module02.TestClass02) ...
Running Test Method : test_case02
ok
```

```
test_case01 (test.test_module03.TestClass03) ...
Running Test Method : test_case01
We're in custom made function : add
ok
test_case02 (test.test_module03.TestClass03) ...
Running Test Method : test_case02
ok
test_case03 (test.test_module03.TestClass03) ...
Running Test Method : test_case03
We're in custom made function : add
```

There are more command-line options for test discovery. You can specify the starting directory with -s or --start-directory. By default, the current directory is the starting directory.

You can use -p or --pattern for the filename pattern. test*.py is the default pattern.

You can use -t or --top-level-directory to specify the top-level directory of the project. The default value for this is the start directory.

As you can see in the verbose output, the unittest automatically found and ran all the test modules located in the chapter03 directory and its subdirectories. This saves you the pain of running each test module separately and collecting the results individually. Test discovery is one of the most important features of any automation testing framework.

Coding Conventions for unittest

As you have seen, test discovery automatically finds and runs all the tests in a project directory. To achieve this effect, you need to follow some coding and naming conventions for your test code. You may have noticed already that I have consistently followed these conventions in all the code examples in this book.

- In order to be compatible with test discovery, all of the test files must be either modules or packages importable from the top-level directory of the project.

- By default, test discovery always starts from the current directory.

- By default, test discovery always searches for test*.py patterns in the filenames.

Assertions in unittest

You have learned about a few basic assertions, like assertEqual() and assertTrue(). The following tables list the most used assertions and their purpose.

Method	Checks That
assertEqual(a, b)	a == b
assertNotEqual(a, b)	a != b
assertTrue(x)	bool(x) is True
assertFalse(x)	bool(x) is False
assertIs(a, b)	a is b
assertIsNot(a, b)	a is not b
assertIsNone(x)	x is None
assertIsNotNone(x)	x is not None
assertIn(a, b)	a in b
assertNotIn(a, b)	a not in b

(continued)

Method	Checks That
assertIsInstance(a, b)	isinstance(a, b)
assertNotIsInstance(a, b)	not isinstance(a, b)
assertAlmostEqual(a, b)	round(a-b, 7) == 0
assertNotAlmostEqual(a, b)	round(a-b, 7) != 0
assertGreater(a, b)	a > b
assertGreaterEqual(a, b)	a >= b
assertLess(a, b)	a < b
assertLessEqual(a, b)	a <= b
assertRegexpMatches(s, r)	r.search(s)
assertNotRegexpMatches(s, r)	not r.search(s)
assertItemsEqual(a, b)	sorted(a) == sorted(b)
assertDictContainsSubset(a, b)	all the key/value pairs in a exist in b

Method	Used to Compare
assertMultiLineEqual(a, b)	Strings
assertSequenceEqual(a, b)	Sequences
assertListEqual(a, b)	Lists
assertTupleEqual(a, b)	Tuples
assertSetEqual(a, b)	sets or frozensets
assertDictEqual(a, b)	Dicts

All the assert methods listed in the previous table are good enough for most programmers and testers when automating tests.

Other Useful Methods

This section looks at a few useful methods that will help you debug and understand the flow of execution.

The id() and shortDescription() methods are very useful for debugging. id() returns the name of the method and shortDescription() returns the description of the method. Listing 3-16 shows an example.

Listing 3-16. test_module10.py

```python
import unittest
class TestClass11(unittest.TestCase):
    def test_case01(self):
        """This is a test method..."""
        print("\nIn test_case01()")
        print(self.id())
        print(self.shortDescription())
```

The output of Listing 3-16 is as follows:

```
test_case01 (test_module10.TestClass11)
This is a test method... ...
In test_case01()
test_module10.TestClass11.test_case01
This is a test method...
ok
------------------------------------------------------------

Ran 1 test in 0.002s
OK
```

Failing a Test

Many times, you might want to have a method that explicitly fails a test when it's called. In unittest, the fail() method is used for that purpose. Check the code in Listing 3-17 as an example.

Listing 3-17. test_module11.py

```
import unittest
class TestClass12(unittest.TestCase):
    def test_case01(self):
        """This is a test method..."""
        print(self.id())
        self.fail()
```

The output of Listing 3-17 is as follows:

```
test_case01 (test_module11.TestClass12)
This is a test method... ...
test_module11.TestClass12.test_case01
FAIL

==========================================================
FAIL: test_case01 (test_module11.TestClass12)
This is a test method...
----------------------------------------------------------
Traceback (most recent call last):
   File "/home/pi/book/code/chapter03/test/test_module11.py",
   line 9, in test_case01
    self.fail()
AssertionError: None
----------------------------------------------------------
Ran 1 test in 0.004s
FAILED (failures=1)
Skipping tests
```

unittest provides a mechanism for skipping tests, conditionally or unconditionally.

It uses the following decorators for implementing the skipping mechanism:

- `unittest.skip(reason)`: Unconditionally skips the decorated test. `reason` should describe why the test is being skipped.

- `unittest.skipIf(condition, reason)`: Skips the decorated test if `condition` is true.

- `unittest.skipUnless(condition, reason)`: Skips the decorated test unless `condition` is true.

- `unittest.expectedFailure()`: Marks the test as an expected failure. If the test fails when it runs, the test is not counted as a failure.

The code in Listing 3-18 demonstrates how to skip tests conditionally and unconditionally.

Listing 3-18. test_module12.py

```
import sys
import unittest

class TestClass13(unittest.TestCase):

    @unittest.skip("demonstrating unconditional skipping")
    def test_case01(self):
        self.fail("FATAL")

    @unittest.skipUnless(sys.platform.startswith("win"),
    "requires Windows")
    def test_case02(self):
        # Windows specific testing code
        pass
```

```
@unittest.skipUnless(sys.platform.startswith("linux"),
"requires Linux")
def test_case03(self):
  # Linux specific testing code
  pass
```

When you run the code in Listing 3-18 on the Linux platform, the output is as follows:

```
test_case01 (test_module12.TestClass13) ... skipped
'demonstrating unconditional skipping'
test_case02 (test_module12.TestClass13) ... skipped 'requires
Windows'
test_case03 (test_module12.TestClass13) ... ok
----------------------------------------------------------
Ran 3 tests in 0.003s
OK (skipped=2)
```

When you run the code in Listing 3-18 on the Windows platform, the output is as follows:

```
test_case01 (test_module12.TestClass13) ... skipped
'demonstrating unconditional skipping'

test_case02 (test_module12.TestClass13) ... ok
test_case03 (test_module12.TestClass13) ... skipped
'requires Linux'
----------------------------------------------------------
Ran 3 tests in 0.003s
OK (skipped=2)
```

As you can see, the code skips the test cases based on the OS where it runs. This trick is very useful for running platform-specific test cases.

You can also skip entire test classes in a test module using the unittest. skip(reason) decorator.

Exceptions in Test Cases

When an exception is raised in a test case, the test case fails. The code shown in Listing 3-19 will raise an exception explicitly.

Listing 3-19. test_module13.py

```
import unittest

class TestClass14(unittest.TestCase):
    def test_case01(self):
        raise Exception
```

The output of Listing 3-19 is as follows:

```
test_case01 (test_module13.TestClass14) ... ERROR

==========================================================
ERROR: test_case01 (test_module13.TestClass14)
----------------------------------------------------------
Traceback (most recent call last):
    File "/home/pi/book/code/chapter03/test/test_module13.py",
    line 6, in test_case01
    raise Exception
Exception
----------------------------------------------------------
Ran 1 test in 0.004s
FAILED (errors=1)
```

The failure message shown when the test fails due to an exception is different from when the test fails due to an assertion.

assertRaises( )

You learned that assert methods are used to check test conditions. The assertRaises() method is used to check if the code block raises the exception mentioned in assertRaises(). If the code raises the exception then the test passes; otherwise, it fails. The code shown in Listing 3-20 demonstrates the use of assertRaises() in detail.

Listing 3-20. test_module14.py

```
import unittest
class Calculator:
    def add1(self, x, y):
        return x + y

    def add2(self, x, y):
        number_types = (int, float, complex)
        if isinstance(x, number_types) and isinstance
        (y, number_ types):
        return x + y
        else:
        raise ValueError

calc = 0
class TestClass16(unittest.TestCase):
    @classmethod
    def setUpClass(cls):
        global calc
        calc = Calculator()

    def setUp(self):
        print("\nIn setUp()...")
```

```
    def test_case01(self):
        self.assertEqual(calc.add1(2, 2), 4)

    def test_case02(self):
        self.assertEqual(calc.add2(2, 2), 4)

    def test_case03(self):
        self.assertRaises(ValueError, calc.add1, 2, 'two')

    def test_case04(self):
        self.assertRaises(ValueError, calc.add2, 2, 'two')

    def tearDown(self):
        print("\nIn tearDown()...")

    @classmethod
    def tearDownClass(cls):
        global calc
        del calc
```

The code in Listing 3-20 defined a class called Calculator that has two
different methods for the addition operation. The add1() method does not
have a provision to raise an exception if a non-numeric argument is passed
to it. The add2() method raises a ValueError if any of the arguments are
non-numeric. Here is the output of the code in Listing 3-20:

```
test_case01 (test_module14.TestClass16) ...
In setUp()...

In tearDown()...
ok
test_case02 (test_module14.TestClass16) ...
In setUp()...

In tearDown()... ok
test_case03 (test_module14.TestClass16) ...
In setUp()...
```

```
In tearDown()...
ERROR
test_case04 (test_module14.TestClass16) ...
In setUp()...

In tearDown()...
ok

==================================================================
ERROR: test_case03 (test_module14.TestClass16)
------------------------------------------------------------------
Traceback (most recent call last):
   File "/home/pi/book/code/chapter03/test/test_module14.py",
   line 37, in test_case03
   self.assertRaises(ValueError, calc.add1, 2, 'two')
   File "/usr/lib/python3.4/unittest/case.py", line 704, in
   assertRaises
   return context.handle('assertRaises', callableObj,
   args, kwargs)
   File "/usr/lib/python3.4/unittest/case.py", line 162, in
   handle callable_obj(*args, **kwargs)
   File "/home/pi/book/code/chapter03/test/test_module14.py",
   line 7, in add1
   return x + y

TypeError: unsupported operand type(s) for +: 'int' and 'str'
------------------------------------------------------------------
Ran 4 tests in 0.030s
FAILED (errors=1)
```

In the output, the test_Case03() fails because add1() does not have a provision to raise an exception when you pass it a non-numeric argument (a string, in this case). assertRaises() is very useful in writing negative test cases, such as when you need to check the behavior of the API against invalid arguments.

Creating Test Suites

You can create your own custom test suites and test runners to run those test suites. The code is presented in Listing 3-21.

Listing 3-21. test_module16.py

```python
import unittest

def setUpModule():
    """called once, before anything else in this module"""
    print("In setUpModule()...")

def tearDownModule():
    """called once, after everything else in this module"""
    print("In tearDownModule()...")

class TestClass06(unittest.TestCase):

    @classmethod
    def setUpClass(cls):
        """called once, before any test"""
        print("In setUpClass()...")

    @classmethod
    def tearDownClass(cls):
        """called once, after all tests, if setUpClass
        successful"""
        print("In tearDownClass()...")

    def setUp(self):
        """called multiple times, before every test method"""
        print("\nIn setUp()...")
```

```
def tearDown(self):
    """called multiple times, after every test method"""
    print("In tearDown()...")

def test_case01(self):
    self.assertTrue("PYTHON".isupper())
    print("In test_case01()")

def test_case02(self):
    self.assertFalse("python".isupper())
    print("In test_case02()")

def suite():
    test_suite = unittest.TestSuite()
    test_suite.addTest(unittest.makeSuite(TestClass06))
    return test_suite

if __name__ == '__main__':
    mySuit=suite()
    runner=unittest.TextTestRunner()
    runner.run(mySuit)
```

This code example created a suite that created an object for unittest .TestSuite(). Then it added the test class to this object with the addTest() method. You can add multiple test classes to that. You can also create multiple test suites like that. Finally, this example is creating an object of this test suite class in the main section. It also creates a testrunner object and then calls that object to run the object of the test suite. You can create multiple test suites and create their objects in the main section. Then you can use the testrunner object to call the objects of those test suites.

Creating Test Suites

EXERCISE 3-1
---

unittest, like all the other Python libraries, is too vast a topic to be covered in a single book. So, I recommend you complete the following exercises to gain more knowledge and experience with unittest.

1. Visit the Python 3 Documentation page for unittest at

    `https://docs.python.org/3/library/unittest.html`.

2. Practice all the assertion methods mentioned in this chapter by writing tests using each one of them.

3. Practice using the `unittest.skipIf(condition, reason)` and `unittest.expectedFailure()` decorators. Write code to demonstrate their functionality.

4. Write a test module with multiple test classes and skip an entire test class using the `unittest.skip(reason)` decorator.

5. Experiment with raising exceptions in the test fixtures.

Hint   Try to run the code in Listing 3-22 by enabling each commented-out `raise Exception` line, one line at a time. This will help you understand how an individual fixture behaves when you raise an exception in it.

Listing 3-22. test_module15.py import unittest

```
def setUpModule():
#     raise Exception
      pass
```

```
def tearDownModule():
#      raise Exception
       pass
class TestClass15(unittest.TestCase):
    @classmethod
    def setUpClass(cls):
#      raise Exception
       pass

    def setUp(self):
#      raise Exception
       pass

    def test_case01(self):
       self.id()

    def tearDown(self):
#      raise Exception
       pass

    @classmethod
    def tearDownClass(cls):
#      raise Exception
       Pass
```

Conclusion

In this chapter, you learned about several important concepts, including test fixtures, test classes, test methods, test modules, and test suites. You also learned how to implement all these concepts with unittest. You also learned assertions and automated test discovery. Almost all the concepts you learned in this chapter will be revisited in later chapters that cover other Python testing frameworks. The next chapter looks at nose and `nose2`, which are two other popular Python test automation and test runner frameworks.

All the concepts we learned in this chapter are the foundations of the area of unit test automation. We will be using them throughout this book and these concepts are very useful at work for professional testers and developers.

CHAPTER 4

nose and nose2

The last chapter introduced xUnit and unittest. In this chapter, you will explore yet another unit-testing API for Python, called nose. Its tagline is *nose extends unittest to make testing easier.*

You can use nose's API to write and run automated tests. You can also use nose to run tests written in other frameworks like unittest. This chapter also explores the next actively developed and maintained iteration of nose, nose2.

Introduction to nose

nose is not part of Python's standard library. You have to install it in order to use it. The next section shows how to install it on Python 3.

Installing nose on Linux Distributions

The easiest way to install nose on a Linux computer is to install it using Python's package manager pip. Pip stands for *pip installs packages*. It's a recursive acronym. If pip is not installed on your Linux computer, you can install it by using a system package manager. On any Debian/Ubuntu or derivative computer, install pip with the following command:

```
sudo apt-get install python3-pip
```

© Ashwin Pajankar 2022
A. Pajankar, *Python Unit Test Automation*, https://doi.org/10.1007/978-1-4842-7854-3_4

On Fedora/CentOS and derivatives, run the following commands (assuming you have Python 3.5 installed on the OS) to install pip:

```
sudo yum install python35-setuptools
sudo easy_install pip
```

Once pip is installed, you can install nose with the following command:

```
sudo pip3 install nose
```

Installing nose on macOS and Windows

pip is preinstalled with Python 3 on macOS and Windows. Install nose with the following command:

```
pip3 install nose
```

Verifying the Installation

Once nose is installed, run the following command to verify the installation:

```
nosetests -V
```

It will show output as follows:

```
nosetests version 1.3.7
```

On Windows, this command may return error, so you can use the following command alternatively:

```
python -m nose -V
```

Getting Started with nose

To get started with nose, follow the same path of exploration that you followed with unittest. Create a directory called chapter04 in the code directory and copy the mypackage directory from the chapter03 directory to code. You will need it later. Create a directory called test too. After all this, the chapter04 directory structure should look like the structure shown in Figure 4-1.

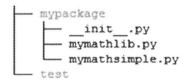

Figure 4-1. *The chapter04 directory structure*

Save all the code examples to the test directory only.

A Simple nose Test Case

A very simple nose test case is demonstrated in Listing 4-1.

Listing 4-1. test_module01.py

```
def test_case01():
    assert 'aaa'.upper() == 'AAA'
```

In Listing 4-1, test_case01() is the test function. assert is Python's built-in keyword and it works like the assert methods in unittest. If you compare this code with the simplest test case in the unittest framework, you will notice that you do not have to extend the test from any parent class. This makes the test code cleaner and less cluttered.

If you try to run it with the following commands, it will not yield any output:

```
python3 test_module01.py
python3 test_module01.py -v
```

This is because you have not included a test-runner in the code.

You can run it by using the -m command-line option for Python, as follows:

```
python3 -m nose test_module01.py
```

The output is as follows:

```
.
------------------------------------------------------------
Ran 1 test in 0.007s
OK
```

Verbose mode can be invoked by adding the -v command-line option as follows:

```
python3 -m nose -v test_module01.py
```

The output is as follows:

```
test.test_module01.test_case01 ... ok
------------------------------------------------------------
Ran 1 test in 0.007s
OK
```

Running the Test Module with nosetests

You can use nose's nosetests command to run the test modules as follows:

```
nosetests test_module01.py
```

The output is as follows:

```
.
------------------------------------------------------------
Ran 1 test in 0.006s
OK
```

Verbose mode can be invoked as follows:

```
nosetests test_module01.py -v
```

The output is as follows:

```
test.test_module01.test_case01 ... ok
------------------------------------------------------------
Ran 1 test in 0.007s
OK
```

Using the nosetests command is the simplest way to run test modules. Due to the simplicity and convenience of the coding and invocation style, we will use nosetests to run tests until we introduce and explain nose2. If the command returns an error in Windows, you can invoke the nose module with the Python interpreter.

Getting Help

Use the following commands to get help and documentation about nose:

```
nosetests -h
python3 -m nose -h
```

Organizing the Test Code

In the previous chapter, you learned how to organize the development and testing code of the project in separate directories. You will follow the same standard in this and the next chapter too. First create a test module to test the development code in mypackage. Save the code shown in Listing 4-2 in the test directory.

Listing 4-2. test_module02.py

```
from mypackage.mymathlib import *

class TestClass01:
    def test_case01(self):
        print("In test_case01()")
        assert mymathlib().add(2, 5) == 7
```

Listing 4-2 creates a test class called TestClass01. As discussed earlier, you do not have to extend it from a parent class. The line containing assert checks if the statement mymathlib().add(2, 5) == 7 is true or false to mark the test method as PASS or FAIL.

Also, create an init.py file with the code in Listing 4-3 placed in the test directory.

Listing 4-3. init.py

```
all = ["test_module01", "test_module02"]
```

After this, the chapter04 directory structure will resemble Figure 4-2.

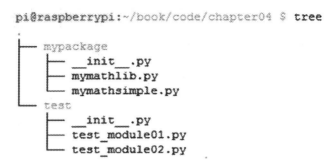

Figure 4-2. *The chapter04 directory structure*

The test package is ready now. You can run the tests from the chapter04 directory as follows:

```
nosetests test.test_module02 -v
```

The output is as follows:

```
test.test_module02.TestClass01.test_case01 ... ok
-----------------------------------------------------------
Ran 1 test in 0.008s
OK
```

The convention for running a specific test class is a bit different in nose. The following is an example:

```
nosetests test.test_module02:TestClass01 -v
```

You can also run an individual test method as follows:

```
nosetests test.test_module02:TestClass01.test_case01 -v
```

97

Test Discovery

You learned about test discovery in an earlier chapter. nose also supports
the test discovery process. In fact, test discovery in nose is even simpler
than in unittest. You do not have to use the discover subcommand
for test discovery. You just need to navigate to the project directory
(chapter04 in this case) and run the nosetests command, as follows:

```
nosetests
```

You can also invoke this process in verbose mode:

```
nosetests -v
```

The output is as follows:

```
test.test_module01.test_case01 ... ok
test.test_module02.TestClass01.test_case01 ... ok
Ran 2 tests in 0.328s
OK
```

As you can see in the output, nosetests automatically discovers the
test package and runs all its test modules.

Fixtures for Classes, Modules, and Methods

nose provides xUnit-style fixtures that behave in similar way as the fixtures
in unittest. Even the names of the fixtures are same. Consider the code in
Listing 4-4.

Listing 4-4. test_module03.py

```python
from mypackage.mymathlib import *

math_obj = 0

def setUpModule():
    """called once, before anything else in this module"""
    print("In setUpModule()...")
    global math_obj
    math_obj = mymathlib()

def tearDownModule():
    """called once, after everything else in this module"""
    print("In tearDownModule()...")
    global math_obj del math_obj
class TestClass02:
    @classmethod
    def setUpClass(cls):
        """called once, before any test in the class"""
        print("In setUpClass()...")

    def setUp(self):
        """called before every test method"""
        print("\nIn setUp()...")

    def test_case01(self):
        print("In test_case01()")
        assert math_obj.add(2, 5) == 7

    def test_case02(self):
        print("In test_case02()")

    def tearDown(self):
        """called after every test method"""
        print("In tearDown()...")
```

```
@classmethod
def tearDownClass(cls):
    """called once, after all tests, if setUpClass()
        successful"""
    print ("\nIn tearDownClass()...")
```

If you run the code in Listing 4-4 with the following command:

```
nosetests test_module03.py -v
```

The output will be as follows:

```
test.test_module03.TestClass02.test_case01 ... ok
test.test_module03.TestClass02.test_case02 ... ok
-----------------------------------------------------------
Ran 2 tests in 0.010s
OK
```

In order to get more details about the test execution, you need to add the -s option to the command line, which allows any stdout output to be printed in the command line immediately.

Run the following command:

```
nosetests test_module03.py -vs
```

The output is as follows:

```
In setUpModule()...
Creating object : mymathlib
In setUpClass()...
test.test_module03.TestClass02.test_case01 ...
In setUp()...
In test_case01()
In tearDown()...
ok
```

```
test.test_module03.TestClass02.test_case02 ...
In setUp()...
In test_case02()
In tearDown()...
ok

In tearDownClass()...
In tearDownModule()...
Destroying object : mymathlib
--------------------------------------------------------------
Ran 2 tests in 0.011s
OK
```

From now on, the examples will add the -s option to the nosetests command while executing the tests.

Fixtures for Functions

Before you get started with the fixtures for functions, you must understand the difference between a function and a method in Python. A *function* is a named piece of code that performs an operation and a *method* is a function with an extra parameter that's the object on which it runs. A function is not associated with a class. A method is always associated with a class.

Check the code in Listing 4-5 as an example.

Listing 4-5. test_module04.py

```
from nose.tools import with_setup

def setUpModule():
    """called once, before anything else in this module"""
    print("\nIn setUpModule()...")
```

101

```
def tearDownModule():
    """called once, after everything else in this module"""
    print("\nIn tearDownModule()...")

def setup_function():
    """setup_function(): use it with @with_setup() decorator"""
    print("\nsetup_function()...")

def teardown_function():
    """teardown_function(): use it with @with_setup()
    decorator"""
    print("\nteardown_function()...")

def test_case01():
    print("In test_case01()...")

def test_case02():
    print("In test_case02()...")

@with_setup(setup_function, teardown_function)
def test_case03():
    print("In test_case03()...")
```

In the code in Listing 4-5, test_case01(), test_case02(), test_case03(), setup_ function(), and teardown_function() are the functions. They are not associated with a class. You have to use the @with_setup() decorator, which is imported from nose.tools, to assign setup_function() and teardown_function() as fixtures of test_case03(). nose recognizes test_case01(), test_case02(), and test_case03() as test functions because the names begin with test_. setup_function() and teardown_function() are recognized as fixtures of test_case03(), due to the @with_setup() decorator.

The test_case01() and test_case02() functions do not have any fixtures assigned to them.

Let's run this code with the following command:

```
nosetests test_module04.py -vs
```

The output is as follows:

```
In setUpModule()...
test.test_module04.test_case01 ... In test_case01()...
ok
test.test_module04.test_case02 ... In test_case02()...
ok
test.test_module04.test_case03 ... setup_function()...
In test_case03()...

teardown_function()...
ok

In tearDownModule()...
------------------------------------------------------------
Ran 3 tests in 0.011s
OK
```

As you can see in the output, setup_function() and
teardown_function() run before and after test_case03(), respectively.
unittest does not have a provision for the fixtures at the test function
level. Actually, unittest does not support the concept of standalone test
functions, as everything has to be extended from the TestCase class and a
function cannot be extended.

It's not mandatory that you name the function-level fixtures
setup_function() and teardown_function(). You can name them
anything you want (except, of course, for Python 3's reserved keywords).
They will be executed before and after the test function as long as you use
them in the @with_setup() decorator.

Fixtures for Packages

unittest does not have a provision for package-level fixtures. Package fixtures are executed when the test package or part of the test package is invoked. Change the contents of the init.py file in the test directory to the code shown in Listing 4-6.

Listing 4-6. init.py

```
all = ["test_module01", "test_module02", "test_module03",
"test_module04"]

def setUpPackage():
    print("In setUpPackage()...")

def tearDownPackage():
    print("In tearDownPackage()...")
```

If you run a module in this package now, the package-level fixtures will run before beginning any test and after the entire test in the package. Run the following command:

```
nosetests test_module03.py -vs
```

Here is the output:

```
In setUpPackage()...
In setUpModule()...
Creating object : mymathlib
In setUpClass()...
test.test_module03.TestClass02.test_case01 ...
In setUp()...
In test_case01()
In tearDown()...
ok
test.test_module03.TestClass02.test_case02 ...
```

```
In setUp()...
In test_case02() In tearDown()...
ok

In tearDownClass()...
In tearDownModule()...
Destroying object : mymathlib
In tearDownPackage()...
-----------------------------------------------------------

Ran 2 tests in 0.012s
OK
```

Alternate Names of the nose Fixtures

This table lists the alternate names of the nose fixtures.

Fixture	Alternative Name(s)
setUpPackage	setup, setUp, or setup_package
tearDownPackage	teardown, tearDown, or teardown_package
setUpModule	setup, setUp, or setup_module
tearDownModule	teardown, tearDown, or teardown_module
setUpClass	setupClass, setup_class, setupAll, or setUpAll
tearDownClass	teardownClass, teardown_class, teardownAll, or tearDownAll
setUp (class method fixtures)	setup
tearDown (class method fixtures)	Teardown

assert_equals( )

Until now, you have been using Python's built-in keyword assert to check the actual results against expected values. nose has its own assert_equals() method for this. The code in Listing 4-7 demonstrates the use of assert_equals() and assert.

Listing 4-7. test_module05.py

```
from nose.tools import import assert_equals

def test_case01():
    print("In test_case01()...")
    assert 2+2 == 5

def test_case02():
    print("In test_case02()...")
    assert_equals(2+2, 5)
```

Run the code in Listing 4-7. Here is the output:

```
In setUpPackage()...
test.test_module05.test_case01 ... In test_case01()...
FAIL
test.test_module05.test_case02 ... In test_case02()...
FAIL
In tearDownPackage()...


============================================================
FAIL: test.test_module05.test_case01
------------------------------------------------------------
Traceback (most recent call last):
  File "/usr/local/lib/python3.4/dist-packages/nose/case.py",
  line 198, in runTest
  self.test(*self.arg)
```

```
    File "/home/pi/book/code/chapter04/test/test_module05.py",
    line 6, in test_case01
    assert 2+2 == 5
AssertionError
==============================================================
FAIL: test.test_module05.test_case02
--------------------------------------------------------------
Traceback (most recent call last):
    File "/usr/local/lib/python3.4/dist-packages/nose/case.py",
    line 198, in runTest
    self.test(*self.arg)
    File "/home/pi/book/code/chapter04/test/test_module05.py",
    line 11, in test_case02
    assert_equals(2+2, 5)
AssertionError: 4 != 5
--------------------------------------------------------------
Ran 2 tests in 0.013s
FAILED (failures=2)
```

Both test cases failed due to incorrect test inputs. Note the difference between the logs printed by these test methods. In test_case02(), you get more information about the cause of the failure, as you are using nose's assert_equals() method.

Testing Tools

nose.tools has a few methods and decorators that come in very handy when you're automating tests. This section looks at a few of those testing tools.

ok_ and eq_

ok_ and eq_ are shorthand for assert and assert_equals(), respectively. They also come with a parameter for an error message when the test case fails. The code in Listing 4-8 demonstrates this.

Listing 4-8. test_module06.py

```
from nose.tools import ok_, eq_

def test_case01():
    ok_(2+2 == 4, msg="Test Case Failure...")

def test_case02():
    eq_(2+2, 4, msg="Test Case Failure...")

def test_case03():
    ok_(2+2 == 5, msg="Test Case Failure...")

def test_case04():
    eq_(2+2, 5, msg="Test Case Failure...")
```

The following shows the output of the code in Listing 4-8.

```
In setUpPackage()... test.test_module06.test_case01 ... ok
test.test_module06.test_case02 ... ok
test.test_module06.test_case03 ... FAIL
test.test_module06.test_case04 ... FAIL
In tearDownPackage()...

===============================================================
FAIL: test.test_module06.test_case03
---------------------------------------------------------------
Traceback (most recent call last):
  File "/usr/local/lib/python3.4/dist-packages/nose/case.py",
  line 198, in runTest
```

```
    self.test(*self.arg)
    File "/home/pi/book/code/chapter04/test/test_module06.py",
    line 13, in test_case03
    ok_(2+2 == 5, msg="Test Case Failure...")
AssertionError: Test Case Failure...

==============================================================
FAIL: test.test_module06.test_case04
--------------------------------------------------------------
Traceback (most recent call last):
    File "/usr/local/lib/python3.4/dist-packages/nose/case.py",
    line 198, in runTest
    self.test(*self.arg)
    File "/home/pi/book/code/chapter04/test/test_module06.py",
    line 17, in test_case04
    eq_(2+2, 5, msg="Test Case Failure...")
AssertionError: Test Case Failure...
--------------------------------------------------------------

Ran 4 tests in 0.015s
FAILED (failures=2)
```

The @raises( ) Decorator

When you use the raises decorator before the test, it must raise one of
the exceptions mentioned in the list of exceptions associated with the
@raises() decorator. Listing 4-9 demonstrates this idea.

Listing 4-9. test_module07.py

```
from nose.tools import raises

@raises(TypeError, ValueError)
def test_case01():
    raise TypeError("This test passes")
```

```
@raises(Exception)
def test_case02():
    pass
```

The output is as follows:

```
In setUpPackage()...
test.test_module07.test_case01 ... ok
test.test_module07.test_case02 ... FAIL
In tearDownPackage()...

============================================================
FAIL: test.test_module07.test_case02
------------------------------------------------------------
Traceback (most recent call last):
  File "/usr/local/lib/python3.4/dist-packages/nose/case.py",
  line 198, in runTest
  self.test(*self.arg)
  File "/usr/local/lib/python3.4/dist-packages/nose/tools/
  nontrivial.py", line 67, in newfunc
  raise AssertionError(message)
AssertionError: test_case02() did not raise Exception
------------------------------------------------------------
Ran 2 tests in 0.012s
FAILED (failures=1)
```

As you can see, test_case02() fails, as it does not raise an exception when it is supposed to. You can cleverly use this to write negative test cases.

The @timed( ) decorator

If you are using a timed decorator with the test, the test must finish within the time mentioned in the @timed() decorator to pass. The code in Listing 4-10 demonstrates this idea.

Listing 4-10. test_module10.py

```
from nose.tools import timed
import time

@timed(.1)
def test_case01():
    time.sleep(.2)
```

This test fails, as it takes more time to finish the execution of the test than is allotted in the @timed() decorator. The output of execution is as follows:

```
In setUpPackage()...
test.test_module08.test_case01 ... FAIL
In tearDownPackage()...

==========================================================
FAIL: test.test_module08.test_case01
----------------------------------------------------------
Traceback (most recent call last):
    File "/usr/local/lib/python3.4/dist-packages/nose/case.py",
    line 198, in runTest
    self.test(*self.arg)
    File "/usr/local/lib/python3.4/dist-packages/nose/tools/
    nontrivial.py", line 100, in newfunc
```

```
    raise TimeExpired("Time limit (%s) exceeded" % limit) nose.
    tools.nontrivial.TimeExpired: Time limit (0.1) exceeded
----------------------------------------------------------
Ran 1 test in 0.211s
FAILED (failures=1)
```

It is the collection or group of related tests that can be executed or scheduled to be executed together.

Report Generation

Let's look at the various ways to generate comprehensible reports using nose.

Creating an XML Report

nose has a built-in feature for generating XML reports. These are xUnit-style formatted reports. You have to use --with-xunit to generate the report. The report is generated in the current working directory.

Run the following command in the test directory:

```
nosetests test_module01.py -vs --with-xunit
```

The output will be as follows:

```
In setUpPackage()...
test.test_module01.test_case01 ... ok
In tearDownPackage()...
----------------------------------------------------------
XML: /home/pi/book/code/chapter04/test/nosetests.xml
----------------------------------------------------------
Ran 1 test in 0.009s
OK
```

The generated XML file is shown in Listing 4-11.

Listing 4-11. nosetests.xml

```
<?xml version="1.0" encoding="UTF-8"?>
<testsuite name="nosetests" tests="1" errors="0" failures="0"
skip="0">
<testcase classname="test.test_module01" name="test_case01"
time="0.002">
</testcase>
</testsuite>
```

Creating an HTML Report

nose does not have a built-in provision for HTML reports. You have to install a plugin for that. Run the following command to install the HTML output plugin:

```
sudo pip3 install nose-htmloutput
```

Once the plugin is installed, you can run the following command to execute the test:

```
nosetests test_module01.py -vs --with-html
```

Here is the output:

```
In setUpPackage()...
test.test_module01.test_case01 ... ok
In tearDownPackage()...
-------------------------------------------------------------
HTML: nosetests.html
-------------------------------------------------------------
Ran 1 test in 0.009s
OK
```

The plugin saves the output in the current location in a file called `nosetests.html`.

Figure 4-3 shows a snapshot of the `nosetests.html` file, opened in a web browser.

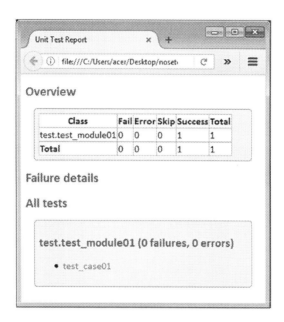

Figure 4-3. *The nosetests.html file*

Creating Color Output in the Console

Until now, you saw methods that generate formatted output files. While running `nosetest`, you must have observed that the console output is monochrome (white text on a dark background and vice versa). The plugin called `rednose` is used to create colored console output. You can install that plugin using the following command:

```
sudo pip3 install rednose
```

Once the plugin is installed, run the following command:

```
nosetests test_module08.py -vs --rednose
```

Figure 4-4 shows a screenshot of the output, although you won't see it in color here, due to the grayscale nature of the published book.

```
pi@raspberrypi:~/book/code/chapter04/test $ nosetests test_module08.py -vs --rednose
In setUpPackage()...
test.test_module08.test_case01 ... FAILED
In tearDownPackage()...
----------------------------------------------------------------------
1) FAIL: test.test_module08.test_case01
----------------------------------------------------------------------
   Traceback (most recent call last):
                                                           line 198 in runTest
      self.test(*self.arg)
                                                           line 100 in newfunc
      raise TimeExpired("Time limit (%s) exceeded" % limit)
   TimeExpired: Time limit (0.1) exceeded


1 test run in 0.224 seconds.
1 FAILED (0 tests passed)
```

Figure 4-4. *A rednose demo*

Running unittest Tests from nose

In the beginning of the chapter, you read that you can run unittest tests with nose. Let's try that now. Navigate to the chapter03 directory. Run the following command to discover and execute all of the unittest tests automatically:

```
nosetests -v
```

This is the output:

```
test_case01 (test.test_module01.TestClass01) ... ok
test_case02 (test.test_module01.TestClass01) ... ok
test_case01 (test.test_module02.TestClass02) ... ok
test_case02 (test.test_module02.TestClass02) ... ok
test_case01 (test.test_module03.TestClass03) ... ok
```

```
test_case02 (test.test_module03.TestClass03) ... ok
test_case03 (test.test_module03.TestClass03) ... FAIL
test_case04 (test.test_module03.TestClass03) ... FAIL
test_case01 (test.test_module04.TestClass04) ... ok
```

I am truncating the output as it would otherwise fill many pages. Run the command yourself to see the entire output.

Running doctest Tests from nose

You can run doctest test from nose as follows. First navigate to the directory where you saved the doctest tests:

```
cd ~/book/code/chapter02
```

Then run the tests as follows:

```
nosetests -v
```

The output is as follows:

```
This is test_case01(). ... ok
This is test_function01(). ... ok

----------------------------------------------------------
Ran 2 tests in 0.007s

OK
```

Advantages of nose over unittest

Here is a summary of the advantages of nose over unittest:

- Unlike unittest, nose does not require you to extend test cases from a parent class. This results in less code.

- Using nose, you can write test functions. This is not possible in unittest.

- nose has more fixtures than unittest. In addition to the regular unittest fixtures, nose has package- and function-level fixtures.

- nose has alternate names for fixtures.

- nose.tools offers many features for automating test cases.

- Test discovery is simpler in nose than in unittest, as nose does not need a Python interpreter with the discover subcommand.

- nose can recognize and run unittest tests easily.

Disadvantages of nose

The only and biggest disadvantage of nose is that it is not under active development and has been in maintenance mode for the past several years. It will likely cease without a new person or team to take over its maintenance. If you're planning to start a project and are looking for a suitable automation framework for Python 3, you should use pytest, nose2, or plain unittest.

You might be wondering why I even spent time covering nose if it is not being actively developed. The reason is that learning a more advanced framework like nose helps you understand the limitations of unittest. Also, if you are working with an older project that uses nose as the test automation and/or unit-testing framework, it will help you understand your tests.

Using nose2

nose2 is the next generation of testing for Python. It is based on the plugins branch of unittest2.

nose2 aims to improve on nose in the following ways:

- It provides a better plugin API.

- It is easier for users to configure.

- It simplifies internal interfaces and processes.

- It supports Python 2 and 3 from the same codebase.

- It encourages greater community involvement in its development.

- Unlike nose, it is under active development.

nose2 can be installed conveniently using the following command:

```
sudo pip3 install nose2
```

Once installed, nose2 can be invoked by running nose2 at the command prompt.

It can be used to auto-discover and run the unittest and nose test modules. Run the nose2 -h command at the command prompt to get help with the various nose2 command-line options.

The following are the important differences between nose and nose2:

- Python versions

  nose supports Python version 2.4 and above. nose2 supports pypy, 2.6, 2.7, 3.2, 3.3, 3.4, and 3.5. nose2 does not support all the versions, as it is not possible to support all the Python versions in a single codebase.

- Test loading

  nose loads and executes test modules one by one, which is called *lazy loading*. On the contrary, nose2 loads all the modules first and then executes them all at once.

- Test discovery

  Because of the difference between the test loading techniques, nose2 does not support all the project layouts. The layout shown in Figure 4-5 is supported by nose. However, it will not be loaded correctly by nose2. nose can distinguish between ./dir1/test.py and ./dir1/dir2/test.py.

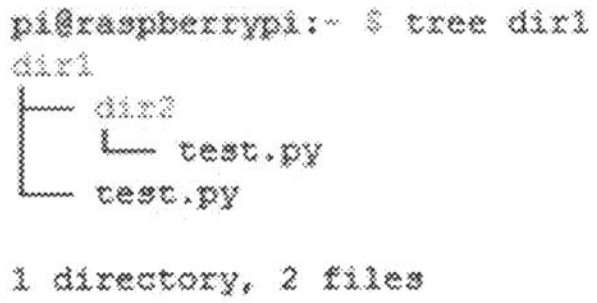

```
pi@raspberrypi:~ $ tree dir1
dir1
├── dir2
│   └── test.py
└── test.py

1 directory, 2 files
```

Figure 4-5. nose2 unsupported test layout

You can run tests with nose2 as follows:

```
nose2 -v
```

You can also parameterize tests, as shown in Listing 4-12.

Listing 4-12. test_module09.py

```
from nose2.tools import params

@params("Test1234", "1234Test", "Dino Candy")
def test_starts_with(value):
    assert value.startswith('Test')
```

You can run the tests as follows:

```
nose2 -v
```

or

```
python -m nose2 test_module09
```

The output is as follows:

```
.FF
================================================================
FAIL: test_module09.test_starts_with:2
'1234Test'
----------------------------------------------------------------
Traceback (most recent call last):
  File "C:\Users\Ashwin\Google Drive\Python Unit
  Test Automation - Second Edition\Code\chapter04\test\
  test_module09.py", line 5, in test_starts_with
    assert value.startswith('Test')
AssertionError

================================================================
FAIL: test_module09.test_starts_with:3
'Dino Candy'
----------------------------------------------------------------
Traceback (most recent call last):
  File "C:\Users\Ashwin\Google Drive\Python Unit Test
  Automation - Second Edition\Code\chapter04\test\
  test_module09.py", line 5, in test_starts_with
    assert value.startswith('Test')
AssertionError

---------------------------------------------------------------
Ran 3 tests in 0.002s

FAILED (failures=2)
```

You can directly launch the test script from any IDE without specifying the nose2 module by modifying the code, as shown in Listing 4-13.

Listing 4-13. test_module20.py

```
from nose2.tools import params

@params("Test1234", "1234Test", "Dino Candy")
def test_starts_with(value):
    assert value.startswith('Test')

if __name__ == '__main__':
    import nose2
    nose2.main()
```

You can launch it directly from any IDE like IDLE and it will produce the same results.

EXERCISE 4-1

Check if the codebase in your organization is using unittest, nose, or nose2. Consult with the owners of the codebase and plan a migration from these frameworks to a better and more flexible unit-testing framework.

Conclusion

In this chapter, you learned about the advanced unit-testing framework, nose. Unfortunately, it is not being developed actively so you need to use nose2 as a test-runner for nose tests. In the next chapter, you learn about and explore an advanced test automation framework called py.test.

CHAPTER 5

pytest

In Chapter 4, you explored nose, which is an advanced and better
framework for Python testing. Unfortunately, nose has not been under
active development for the past several years. That makes it an unsuitable
candidate for a test framework when you want to choose something for a
long-term project. Moreover, there are many projects that use unittest or
nose or a combination of both. You definitely need a framework that has
more features than unittest, and unlike nose, it should be under active
development. nose2 is more of a test-runner for unittest and an almost
defunct tool. You need a unit test framework that's capable of discovering
and running tests written in unittest and nose. It should be advanced
and must be actively developed, maintained, and supported. The answer
is pytest.

This chapter extensively explores a modern, advanced, and better test
automation framework, called pytest. First, you'll learn how pytest offers
traditional xUnit style fixtures and then you will explore the advanced
fixtures offered by pytest.

© Ashwin Pajankar 2022   123
A. Pajankar, *Python Unit Test Automation*, https://doi.org/10.1007/978-1-4842-7854-3_5

Introduction to pytest

pytest is not a part of Python's standard library. You have to install it in order to use it, just like you installed nose and nose2. Let's see how you can install it for Python 3. pytest can be installed conveniently by running the following command in Windows:

```
pip install pytest
```

For Linux and macOS, you install it using pip3 as follows:

```
sudo pip3 install pytest
```

This installs pytest for Python 3. It might show a warning. There will be a directory name in the warning message. I used a Raspberry Pi with Raspberry Pi OS as the Linux system. It uses bash as the default shell. Add the following line to the .bashrc and .bash_profile files in the home directory.

```
PATH=$PATH:/home/pi/.local/bin
```

After adding this line to the files, restart the shell. You can now check the installed version by running the following command:

```
py.test --version
```

The output is as follows:

```
pytest 6.2.5
```

Simple Test

Before you begin, create a directory called chapter05 in the code directory. Copy the mypackage directory as it is from the chapter04 directory. Create a directory called test in chapter05. Save all the code files for this chapter in the test directory.

Just like when using nose, writing a simple test is very easy. See the code in Listing 5-1 as an example.

Listing 5-1. test_module01.py

```
def test_case01():
    assert 'python'.upper() == 'PYTHON'
```

Listing 5-1 imports pytest in the first line. test_case01() is the test function. Recall that assert is a Python built-in keyword. Also, just like with nose, you do not need to extend these tests from any class. This helps keep the code uncluttered.

Run the test module with the following command:

```
python3 -m pytest test_module01.py
```

The output is as follows:

```
===================== test session starts ====================
platform linux -- Python 3.4.2, pytest-3.0.4, py-1.4.31,
pluggy-0.4.0 rootdir: /home/pi/book/code/chapter05/test,
inifile:
collected 1 items

test_module01.py .
================== 1 passed in 0.05 seconds =================
```

You can also use verbose mode:

```
python3 -m pytest -v test_module01.py
```

The output is as follows:

```
=============== test session starts ==========================
platform linux -- Python 3.4.2, pytest-3.0.4, py-1.4.31,
pluggy-0.4.0 --
/usr/bin/python3
```

```
cachedir: .cache
rootdir: /home/pi/book/code/chapter05/test,
inifile: collected 1 items

test_module01.py::test_case01 PASSED


=============== 1 passed in 0.04 seconds ===================
```

Running Tests with the py.test Command

You can also run these tests with pytest's own command, called py.test:

```
py.test test_module01.py
```

The output is as follows:

```
================= test session starts ======================
platform linux -- Python 3.4.2, pytest-3.0.4, py-1.4.31,
pluggy-0.4.0 rootdir: /home/pi/book/code/chapter05/test,
inifile:
collected 1 items

test_module01.py .
=============== 1 passed in 0.04 seconds ==================
```

You can also use verbose mode as follows:

```
py.test test_module01.py -v
```

The output in verbose mode is as follows:

```
=================== test session starts ======================
platform linux -- Python 3.4.2, pytest-3.0.4, py-1.4.31,
pluggy-0.4.0 --
/usr/bin/python3
cachedir: .cache
```

```
rootdir: /home/pi/book/code/chapter05/test,
inifile:
collected 1 items

test_module01.py::test_case01 PASSED
==================== 1 passed in 0.04 seconds =================
```

For the sake of simplicity and convenience, from now onward, you will use the same method to run these tests for rest of this chapter and the book. You will use pytest in the last chapter to implement a project with the methodology of test-driven development. Also, observe when you run your own tests that the output of test execution is in color by default, although the book shows the results in black and white. You do not have to use any external or third-party plugin for this effect. Figure 5-1 shows a screenshot of an execution sample.

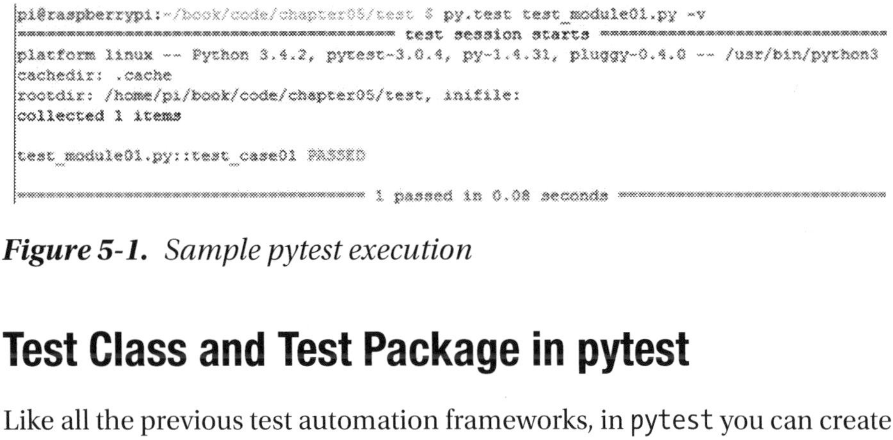

Figure 5-1. *Sample pytest execution*

Test Class and Test Package in pytest

Like all the previous test automation frameworks, in pytest you can create test classes and test packages. Take a look at the code in Listing 5-2 as an example.

Listing 5-2. test_module02.py

```
class TestClass01:

    def test_case01(self):
        assert 'python'.upper() == 'PYTHON'

    def test_case02(self):
        assert 'PYTHON'.lower() == 'python'
```

Also create an init.py file, as shown in Listing 5-3.

Listing 5-3. _init.py

```
all = ["test_module01", "test_module02"]
```

Now navigate to the chapter05 directory:

```
cd /home/pi/book/code/chapter05
```

And run the test package, as follows:

```
py.test test
```

You can see the output by running the previous command. You can also use the following command to run a test package in verbose mode.

```
py.test -v test
```

You can run a single test module within a package with the following command:

```
py.test -v test/test_module01.py
```

You can also run a specific test class as follows:

```
py.test -v test/test_module02.py::TestClass01
```

You can run a specific test method as follows:

```
py.test -v test/test_module02.py::TestClass01::test_case01
```

You can run a specific test function as follows:

```
py.test -v test/test_module01.py::test_case01
```

Test Discovery in pytest

pytest can discover and automatically run the tests, just like unittest, nose, and nose2 can. Run the following command in the project directory to initiate automated test discovery:

```
py.test
```

For verbose mode, run the following command:

```
py.test -v
```

xUnit-Style Fixtures

pytest has xUnit-style fixtures. See the code in Listing 5-4 as an example.

Listing 5-4. test_module03.py

```
def setup_module(module):
    print("\nIn setup_module()...")

def teardown_module(module):
    print("\nIn teardown_module()...")

def setup_function(function):
    print("\nIn setup_function()...")

def teardown_function(function):
    print("\nIn teardown_function()...")
```

```
def test_case01():
    print("\nIn test_case01()...")

 def test_case02():
     print("\nIn test_case02()...")

class TestClass02:

    @classmethod
    def setup_class(cls):
        print ("\nIn setup_class()...")

    @classmethod
    def teardown_class(cls):
        print ("\nIn teardown_class()...")

    def setup_method(self, method):
        print ("\nIn setup_method()...")

    def teardown_method(self, method):
        print ("\nIn teardown_method()...")

    def test_case03(self):
        print("\nIn test_case03()...")

    def test_case04(self):
        print("\nIn test_case04()...")
```

In this code, setup_module() and teardown_module() are module-level fixtures that are invoked before and after anything else in the module. setup_class() and teardown_class() are class-level fixtures and they run before and after anything else in the class. You have to use the @classmethod() decorator with them. setup_method() and teardown_method() are method-level fixtures that run before and after every test method. setup_function() and teardown_function() are function-level fixtures that run before and after every test function in the module. In nose, you need the @with_setup() decorator with the test functions to assign those to the function level-fixtures. In pytest, function-level fixtures are assigned to all test functions by default.

Also, just like with nose, you need to use the -s command-line option to see the detailed log on the command line.

Now run the code with an additional -s option, as follows:

py.test -vs test_module03.py

Next, run the test again with the following command:

py.test -v test_module03.py

Compare the outputs of these modes of execution for a better understanding.

pytest Support for unittest and nose

pytest supports all the tests written in unittest and nose. pytest can automatically discover and run the tests written in unittest and nose. It supports all the xUnit-style fixtures for unittest test classes. It also supports most of the fixtures in nose. Try running py.test -v in the chapter03 and chapter04 directories.

Introduction to pytest Fixtures

Apart from supporting xUnit-style fixtures and unittest fixtures, pytest has its own set of fixtures that are flexible, extensible, and modular. This is one of the core strengths of pytest and why it's a popular choice of automation testers.

In pytest, you can create a fixture and use it as a resource where it is needed.

Consider the code in Listing 5-5 as an example.

Listing 5-5. test_module04.py

```
import pytest

@pytest.fixture()
def fixture01():
    print("\nIn fixture01()...")

def test_case01(fixture01):
    print("\nIn test_case01()...")
```

In Listing 5-5, fixture01() is the fixture function. It is because you are using the @pytest.fixture() decorator with that. test_case01() is a test function that uses fixture01(). For that, you are passing fixture01 as an argument to test_case01().

Here is the output:

```
=================== test session starts ======================
platform linux -- Python 3.4.2, pytest-3.0.4, py-1.4.31,
pluggy-0.4.0 --
/usr/bin/python3
cachedir: .cache
rootdir: /home/pi/book/code/chapter05/test,
inifile: collected 1 items

test_module04.py::test_case01
In fixture01()...

In test_case01()...
PASSED

================= 1 passed in 0.04 seconds ====================
```

As you can see, `fixture01()` is invoked before the test function `test_case01()`. You could also use the `@pytest.mark.usefixtures()` decorator, which achieves the same result. The code in Listing 5-6 is implemented with this decorator and it produces the same output as Listing 5-5.

Listing 5-6. test_module05.py

```python
import pytest

@pytest.fixture() def fixture01():
    print("\nIn fixture01()...")

@pytest.mark.usefixtures('fixture01')
def test_case01(fixture01):
    print("\nIn test_case01()...")
```

The output of Listing 5-6 is exactly the same as the code in Listing 5-5.

You can use the `@pytest.mark.usefixtures()` decorator for a class, as shown in Listing 5-7.

Listing 5-7. test_module06.py

```python
import pytest

@pytest.fixture()
def fixture01():
    print("\nIn fixture01()...")

@pytest.mark.usefixtures('fixture01')
class TestClass03:
    def test_case01(self):
        print("I'm the test_case01")

    def test_case02(self):
        print("I'm the test_case02")
```

Here is the output:

```
================== test session starts ========================
platform linux -- Python 3.4.2, pytest-3.0.4, py-1.4.31,
pluggy-0.4.0 --
/usr/bin/python3
cachedir: .cache
rootdir: /home/pi/book/code/chapter05/test,
inifile: collected 2 items

test_module06.py::TestClass03::test_case01
In fixture01()...

I'm the test_case01
PASSED
test_module06.py::TestClass03::test_case02
In fixture01()...
I'm the test_case02
PASSED

================ 2 passed in 0.08 seconds ====================
```

If you want to run a block of code after a test with a fixture has run,
you have to add a finalizer function to the fixture. Listing 5-8 demonstrates
this idea.

Listing 5-8. test_module07.py

```python
import pytest

@pytest.fixture()
def fixture01(request):
    print("\nIn fixture...")

    def fin():
        print("\nFinalized...")
    request.addfinalizer(fin)
```

```
@pytest.mark.usefixtures('fixture01')
def test_case01():
    print("\nI'm the test_case01")
```

The output is as follows:

```
================= test session starts =======================
platform linux -- Python 3.4.2, pytest-3.0.4, py-1.4.31,
pluggy-0.4.0 --
/usr/bin/python3
 cachedir: .cache
rootdir: /home/pi/book/code/chapter05/test,
inifile: collected 1 items

test_module07.py::test_case01
In fixture...

I'm the test_case01
PASSED
Finalized...

============== 1 passed in 0.05 seconds =====================
```

pytest provides access to the fixture information on the requested object. Listing 5-9 demonstrates this concept.

Listing 5-9. test_module08.py

```
import pytest

@pytest.fixture()
def fixture01(request):
    print("\nIn fixture...")
    print("Fixture Scope: " + str(request.scope))
    print("Function Name: " + str(request.function. name ))
```

```
    print("Class Name: " + str(request.cls))
    print("Module Name: " + str(request.module. name ))
    print("File Path: " + str(request.fspath))

@pytest.mark.usefixtures('fixture01')
def test_case01():
    print("\nI'm the test_case01")
```

The following is the output of Listing 5-9:

```
================== test session starts =======================
platform linux -- Python 3.4.2, pytest-3.0.4, py-1.4.31,
pluggy-0.4.0 --
/usr/bin/python3
 cachedir: .cache
rootdir: /home/pi/book/code/chapter05/test,
inifile:
collected 1 items

test_module08.py::test_case01
In fixture...
Fixture Scope: function
Function Name: test_case01
Class Name: None
Module Name: test.test_module08
File Path: /home/pi/book/code/chapter05/test/test_module08.py

I'm the test_case01
PASSED

============== 1 passed in 0.06 seconds ===================
```

Scope of pytest Fixtures

pytest provides you with a set of scope variables to define exactly when you want to use the fixture. The default scope of any fixture is the function level. It means that, by default, the fixtures are at the level of function.

The following shows the list of scopes for pytest fixtures:

- function: Runs once per test

- class: Runs once per class of tests

- module: Runs once per module

- session: Runs once per session

To use these, define them like this:

```
@pytest.fixture(scope="class")
```

- Use the function scope if you want the fixture to run after every single test. This is fine for smaller fixtures.

- Use the class scope if you want the fixture to run in each class of tests. Typically, you'll group tests that are alike in a class, so this may be a good idea, depending on how you structure things.

- Use the module scope if you want the fixture to run at the start of the current file and then after the file has finished its tests. This can be good if you have a fixture that accesses the database and you set up the database at the beginning of the module and then the finalizer closes the connection.

- Use the session scope if you want to run the fixture at the first test and run the finalizer after the last test has run.

There is no scope for packages in pytest. However, you can cleverly use the session scope as a package-level scope by making sure that only a specific test package runs in a single session.

pytest.raises( )

In unittest, you have assertRaises() to check if any test raises an exception. There is a similar method in pytest. It is implemented as pytest.raises() and is useful for automating negative test scenarios.

Consider the code shown in Listing 5-10.

Listing 5-10. test_module09.py

```
import pytest

def test_case01():
    with pytest.raises(Exception):
        x = 1 / 0

def test_case02():
    with pytest.raises(Exception):
        x = 1 / 1
```

In Listing 5-10, the line with pytest.raises(Exception) checks if an exception is raised in the code. If an exception is raised in the block of code that include the exception, the test passes; otherwise, it fails.

Here is Listing 5-10's output:

```
============== test session starts ==============================
platform linux -- Python 3.4.2, pytest-3.0.4, py-1.4.31,
pluggy-0.4.0 --
/usr/bin/python3
cachedir: .cache
rootdir: /home/pi/book/code/chapter05/test,
```

```
inifile:
collected 2 items

test_module09.py::test_case01 PASSED
test_module09.py::test_case02 FAILED

=========================== FAILURES ===========================
_____test_case02_____
def test_case02():
   with pytest.raises(Exception):
>      x = 1 / 1
E      Failed: DID NOT RAISE <class 'Exception'>

test_module09.py:10: Failed
============== 1 failed, 1 passed in 0.21 seconds =============
```

In test_case01(), an exception is raised, so it passes. test_case02() does not raise an exception, so it fails. As mentioned earlier, this is extremely useful for testing negative scenarios.

Important pytest Command-Line Options

Some of pytest's more important command-line options are discussed in the following sections.

Help

For help, run **py.test -h**. It will display a list with uses of various command-line options.

Stopping After the First (or N) Failures

You can stop the execution of tests after the first failure using `py.test -x`. In the same way, you can use `py.test --maxfail=5` to stop execution after five failures. You can also change the argument provided to `--maxfail`.

Profiling Test Execution Duration

Profiling means assessing execution of programs for factors like time, space, and memory. Profiling is primarily done to improve programs so that they consume fewer resources while executing. The test modules and suites you write are basically programs that test other programs. You can find the slowest tests with `pytest`. You can use the `py.test --durations=10` command to show the slowest tests. You can change the argument provided to `--duration`. Try running this command on the `chapter05` directory as an example.

JUnit-Style Logs

Frameworks like JUnit (a unit test automation framework for Java) produce the logs for execution in XML format. You can generate JUnit-style XML log files for your tests by running the following command:

```
py.test --junitxml=result.xml
```

The XML file will be generated in the current directory.

Conclusion

The following are the reasons I use `pytest` and recommend that all Python enthusiasts and professionals use it:

- It is better than unittest. The resulting code is cleaner and simpler.

- Unlike with nose, pytest is still under active development.

- It has great features for controlling test execution.

- It can generate XML results without an additional plugin.

- It can run unittest tests.

- It has its own set of advanced fixtures that are modular in nature.

If you are working on a project that uses unittest, nose, or doctest as the test framework for Python, I recommend migrating your tests to pytest.

CHAPTER 6

Testing with Selenium

In the last chapter, you became acquainted with a unit test framework, pytest. You should now be somewhat comfortable with writing unit tests with the pytest framework. In this chapter, you learn about the webdriver framework called Selenium.

Introduction to Selenium

Selenium is a webdriver framework. It is used for browser automation. It means that you can open a browser program (or a browser app) programmatically. All the browser operations that you perform manually can be performed programmatically with webdriver frameworks. Selenium is the most popular webdriver framework that is used for browser automation.

Jason Huggins developed Selenium in 2004 as a tool at ThoughtWorks. It was intended to be for internal usage in the organization. After the tool became popular, many people joined its development and it was made open source. Its development continued thereafter as open source. Huggins joined Google in 2007 and continued with the development of the tool.

The name *Selenium* is a joke played on Mercury Interactive, which also created proprietary tools for test automation. The joke is that Mercury poisoning can be cured by Selenium, so the new open source framework was named Selenium. Selenium and Mercury are both elements on the Periodic table.

© Ashwin Pajankar 2022
A. Pajankar, *Python Unit Test Automation*, https://doi.org/10.1007/978-1-4842-7854-3_6

Simon Stewart at ThoughtWorks developed a browser automation tool called WebDriver. The developers at ThoughtWorks and Google met at the Google Test Automation Conference in 2009 and decided to merge the Selenium and Webdriver projects. The new framework was christened Selenium Webdriver or Selenium 2.0.

Selenium has three major components:

- Selenium IDE

- Selenium Webdriver

- Selenium Grid

You will read about Selenium IDE and Selenium Webdriver in this chapter.

Selenium IDE

Selenium IDE is a browser plugin used to record browser actions. After recording, you can play back the entire sequence of actions. You can also export the scripted actions as a code file in various programming languages. Let's get started by installing the plugin on the Chrome and Firefox browsers.

Add the extension to the Chrome web browser with the following URL:

```
https://chrome.google.com/webstore/detail/selenium-ide/
mooikfkahbdckldjjndioackbalphokd
```

Once it's been added, you can access it from the menu next to the address bar, as shown in Figure 6-1.

Figure 6-1. *Selenium IDE for Chrome*

You can access the add-on for the Firefox browser from the following URL:

`https://addons.mozilla.org/en-GB/firefox/addon/selenium-ide/`

Once you add it, you can access it from the menu next to the address bar, as shown in the top-right corner of Figure 6-2.

Figure 6-2. *Selenium IDE for Chrome*

Clicking these options in the respective browser opens a window, as shown in Figure 6-3.

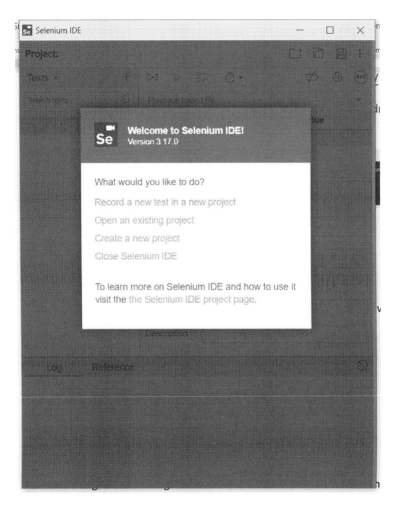

Figure 6-3. *Selenium IDE window*

The GUI for the Selenium IDE is same for all browsers. Click Create a New Project to open a new window, as shown in Figure 6-4.

CHAPTER 6   TESTING WITH SELENIUM

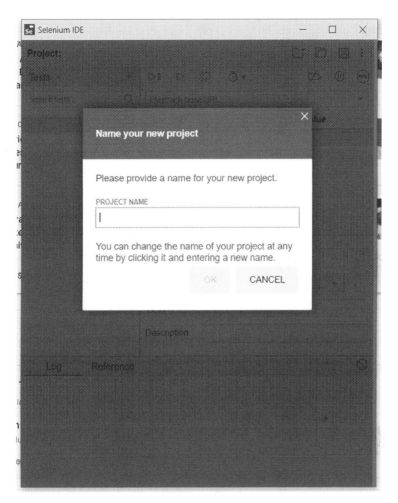

Figure 6-4. *Selenium new project*

Enter a name of your choice. This will enable the OK button. Click the OK button to show the window in Figure 6-5.

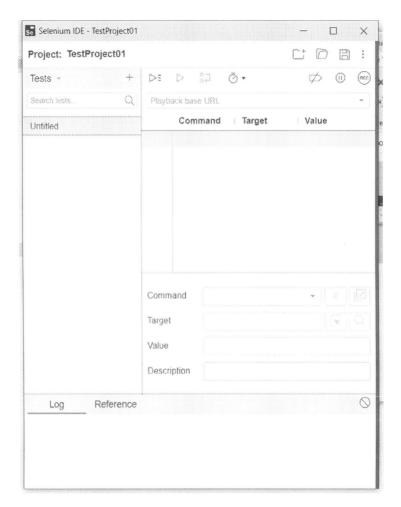

Figure 6-5. *Selenium IDE window*

As you can see, this window is divided into various sections. In the top left, you can see the name of the project. In the top right, you have three icons. The first icon creates a new project when clicked. The second icon is for opening an existing project. The third icon saves the current project. The saved file has a `*.side` extension (Selenium IDE).

Let's rename the existing test. Check the left tab. You can see an untitled test, as shown in Figure 6-6.

148

Figure 6-6. *Renaming the untitled test*

When you save the project, it tries to save it as a new file. You have to save it with the existing name by overwriting the earlier file. Now, click the Record button. The shortcut is Ctrl+U. It opens a new dialog box asking you for the base URL of the project; see Figure 6-7.

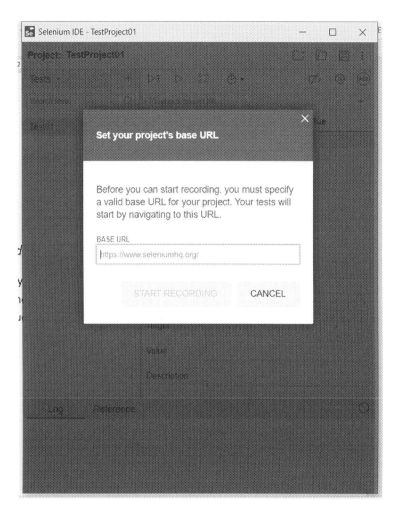

Figure 6-7 *Project Base URL*

You have to enter the URL of the web page to be tested. The URL should also include the text http:// or https://, otherwise it won't consider it a URL. Enter http://www.google.com into the box. It will then enable the Start Recording button. The recording button is red and can be found on the top-right side of the window. Click the button and it will launch a new window with the specified URL. It looks like Figure 6-8.

Figure 6-8. *Selenium IDE recording*

Type **Python** into the search bar and then click Google Search. It will show you the search results. Click the first result and then, after loading the page, close the browser window. Then stop recording by clicking the button from the menu. You will see the recorded steps in the IDE, as shown in Figure 6-9.

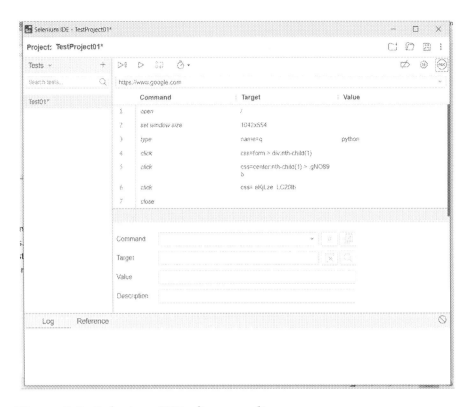

Figure 6-9. *Selenium IDE after recording*

You can automatically rerun all the steps. You can see a group of four icons in the same bar for the Record button. The first icon is to run all the tests and the second is for running the current test. The current project has a single test, so it will run the only test in the suite. Click any of the buttons to automatically repeat this sequence of actions.

This way you can record and execute sequence of actions. Once the recorded tests execute successfully, the bottom section will show the log, as shown in Figure 6-10.

Log	Reference	⊘
4. click on css=form > div:nth-child(1) OK		18:56:04
5. click on css=center:nth-child(1) > .gNO89b OK		18:56:05
6. click on css=.eKjLze .LC20lb OK		18:56:05
7. close OK		18:56:10
'Test01' completed successfully		18:56:10

Figure 6-10. *Selenium IDE logs*

You can add new tests to the project by clicking the + icon in the menu.
A project will usually have multiple tests. Now you learn how to export
your project. You can right-click the test to open a menu, as shown in
Figure 6-6. Click the Export option. It opens a new window, as shown in
Figure 6-11.

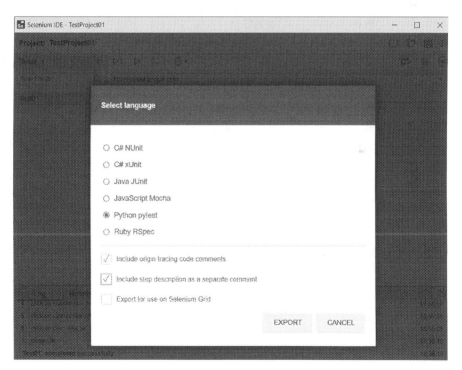

Figure 6-11. *Exporting the project as code*

153

Check the top two options and then click the Export button. It will open a window called Save As. Provide the details and it will save the project as a Python file with the *.py extension in the specified directory. The generated code is shown in Listing 6-1.

Listing 6-1. test_test01.py

```python
# Generated by Selenium IDE
import pytest
import time
import json
from selenium import webdriver
from selenium.webdriver.common.by import By
from selenium.webdriver.common.action_chains import
ActionChains
from selenium.webdriver.support import expected_conditions
from selenium.webdriver.support.wait import WebDriverWait
from selenium.webdriver.common.keys import Keys
from selenium.webdriver.common.desired_capabilities import
DesiredCapabilities

class TestTest01():
  def setup_method(self, method):
    self.driver = webdriver.Chrome()
    self.vars = {}

  def teardown_method(self, method):
    self.driver.quit()

  def test_test01(self):
    # Test name: Test01
    # Step # | name | target | value
    # 1 | open | / |
    self.driver.get("https://www.google.com/")
```

```
# 2 | setWindowSize | 1042x554 |
self.driver.set_window_size(1042, 554)
# 3 | type | name=q | python
self.driver.find_element(By.NAME, "q").send_keys("python")
# 4 | click | css=form > div:nth-child(1) |
self.driver.find_element(By.CSS_SELECTOR, "form >
div:nth-child(1)").click()
# 5 | click | css=center:nth-child(1) > .gNO89b |
self.driver.find_element(By.CSS_SELECTOR,
"center:nth-child(1) > .gNO89b").click()
# 6 | click | css=.eKjLze .LC20lb |
self.driver.find_element(By.CSS_SELECTOR,
".eKjLze .LC20lb").click()
# 7 | close | |
self.driver.close()
```

This is how you can export automated tests to Python. You can run this file with the unittest framework to reproduce the tests later. Don't execute the code yet, as you have not installed the Selenium framework for Python. You will analyze and learn to write your own code in the next section.

Selenium Webdriver

Selenium IDE is a plugin. It is just a record and playback tool with a little provision to customize test cases. If you want full control over your tests, you should be able to write them from scratch. Selenium Webdriver allows you to do that.

The code exported in the last section uses webdriver for browser automation. Here, you see how to write your own code from scratch. You can install Selenium Webdriver with the following command:

```
pip3 install selenium
```

Now you can run the code saved in the last section.

Let's look at how to write the code from scratch. Check out the code in Listing 6-2.

Listing 6-2. prog00.py

```
from selenium import webdriver
driver_path=r'D:\\drivers\\geckodriver.exe'
driver = webdriver.Firefox(executable_path=driver_path)
driver.close()
```

Consider this code line-by-line. The first line imports the library to your program. The second line defines a string. The string contains the path to the driver executable for the browser you are about to automate. You can download the drivers for the various browsers from the following URLs:

```
https://sites.google.com/chromium.org/driver/
https://developer.microsoft.com/en-us/microsoft-edge/tools/
webdriver/
https://github.com/mozilla/geckodriver/releases
```

Visit these web pages and download the appropriate driver for your OS (Windows/Linux/macOS) and architecture (32/64-bit) combination. I downloaded and saved them in a location identified by D:\drivers on my Windows 64-bit OS.

The third line creates a driver object and the fourth line closes it. Launch the program from IDLE or from the command line. It will momentarily open the browser and close it. If you use IDLE, it will also open the geckodriver.exe file separately and you will have to close it manually. You will see how to terminate it programmatically shortly. For now, close it manually. Check out Listing 6-3.

Listing 6-3. prog01.py

```
from selenium import webdriver
driver_path=r'D:\\drivers\\chromedriver.exe'
driver = webdriver.Chrome(executable_path=driver_path)
driver.close()
driver.quit()
```

Here, you are using the Chrome driver and closing the driver executable in the last line. Run this to see the code in action. Next, let's experiment with the edge browser and add some waiting time into the code. Check out Listing 6-4.

Listing 6-4. prog02.py

```
from selenium import webdriver
import time
driver_path=r'D:\\drivers\\msedgedriver.exe'
driver = webdriver.Edge(executable_path=driver_path)
time.sleep(10)
driver.close()
time.sleep(5)
driver.quit()
```

Run the code to see it in action.

You can also write the code for the Safari Browser. Safari webdriver comes preinstalled in macOS. It can be found at `/usr/bin/safaridriver`. You can enable it with the following shell command:

```
safaridriver -enable
```

You can create the driver object with the following line of code in Python:

```
driver = webdriver.Safari()
```

Selenium with Unittest

You can use Selenium framework with `unittest`. This way you can create separate tests for separate cases. You can track the progress of your tests this way. See Listing 6-5.

Listing 6-5. test_test02.py

```python
import unittest
from selenium import webdriver

class TestClass01(unittest.TestCase):

    def setUp(self):
        driver_path=r'D:\\drivers\\geckodriver.exe'
        driver = webdriver.Firefox(executable_path=driver_path)
        self.driver = driver
        print ("\nIn setUp()...")

    def tearDown(self):
        print ("\nIn tearDown")
        self.driver.close()
        self.driver.quit()
```

```
    def test_case01(self):
        print("\nIn test_case01()...")
        self.driver.get("http://www.python.org")
        assert self.driver.title == "Welcome to Python.org"

if __name__ == "__main__":
    unittest.main()
```

This script is creating the webdriver object, opening a web page and checking its title, and when it's done, it closes the browser window and the webdriver. Run the script to see it all in action.

Conclusion

In this chapter, you studied the basics of web browser automation with Selenium. You also learned about the Selenium IDE and how to combine unittest with Selenium.

The next chapter is dedicated to the logging mechanisms in Python.

CHAPTER 7

Logging in Python

In the last chapter, you became acquainted with a unit test framework, Selenium. This chapter is a change of pace and you learn about a related topic, logging.

The chapter covers the following:

- Logging basics

- Logging with an OS

- Manually logging with file operations

- Logging in Python

- Logging with `loguru`

After reading this chapter, you will be more comfortable logging in Python.

Logging Basics

The process of recording something is known as *logging*. For example, if I am recording the temperature, that is known as temperature logging, which is an example of physical logging. We can use this concept in computer programming as well. Many times, you'll get an intermediate output on the terminal. It is used for the purpose of debugging when the program runs. Sometimes programs run automatically using `crontab` (in UNIX-like OSs) or using Windows Scheduler. In such cases, logging is used to determine if there was a problem during execution. Generally,

© Ashwin Pajankar 2022
A. Pajankar, *Python Unit Test Automation*, https://doi.org/10.1007/978-1-4842-7854-3_7

such information is logged to files so that if the maintenance or operations people are not present, they can review the logs at the earliest available opportunity. There are various ways you can log information related to the execution of a program. The following sections look at them one by one.

Logging with an OS

Let's log with an OS using the command line. Consider the program in Listing 7-1.

Listing 7-1. prog00.py

```python
import datetime
import sys
print("Commencing Execution of the program...")
print(datetime.datetime.now())
for i in [1, 2, 3, 4, 5]:
    print("Iteration " + str(i) + " ...")
print("Done...")
print(datetime.datetime.now())
sys.exit(0)
```

When you run this using IDLE or any IDE, you'll see the following output in the terminal:

```
Commencing Execution of the program...
2021-09-01 19:09:14.900123
Iteration 1 ...
Iteration 2 ...
Iteration 3 ...
Iteration 4 ...
Iteration 5 ...
Done...
2021-09-01 19:09:14.901121
```

This is what logging on a terminal looks like. You can also log this in a file. You can use IO redirection in Linux and Windows to achieve this. You can run the program on the Windows command prompt as follows:

```
python prog00.py >> test.log
```

On the Linux terminal, the command is as follows:

```
python3 prog00.py >> test.log
```

This command will create a new file called test.log in the same directory and redirect all the output there.

This is how you can display the execution log and save it in a file.

Manually Logging with File Operations

This section explains how to log events with file operations in Python. First you need to open a file. Use the open() routine to do so. Run the following example from the Python 3 interpreter prompt:

```
>>> logfile = open('mylog.log', 'w')
```

This command creates an object named logfile for the file operations. The first argument to the open() routine is the name of the file and the second operation is the mode in which the file is to be opened. This example uses the w mode, which stands for the write operation. There are many modes for opening files, but this is the only one that's relevant right now. As an exercise, you may explore other modes.

The previous line of code opens the file in write mode if the file exists; otherwise, it creates a new file. Now run the following code:

```
>>> logfile.write('This is the test log.')
```

The output will be as follows:

21

The write() routine writes the given string to the file and returns the length of the string. Finally, you can close the file object as follows:

```
>>> logfile.close()
```

Now, let's modify the earlier script called prog00.py to add the file operations for logging, as shown in Listing 7-2.

Listing 7-2. prog01.py

```
import datetime
import sys
logfile = open('mylog.log', 'w')
msg = "Commencing Execution of the program...\n" +
str(datetime.datetime.now())
print(msg)
logfile.write(msg)
for i in [1, 2, 3, 4, 5]:
    msg = "\nIteration " + str(i) + " ..."
    print(msg)
    logfile.write(msg)
msg = "\nDone...\n" + str(datetime.datetime.now())
logfile.write(msg)
print(msg)
logfile.close()
sys.exit(0)
```

As you can see in Listing 7-2, you are creating strings of the log messages. The program then sends them to the log file and to the terminal at the same time. You can run this program using the IDLE or with the command prompt.

This is how to log the execution of programs manually using file operations.

Logging in Python

This section explains the logging process in Python. You do not have to install anything for this, as it comes with the Python installation as a part of its batteries-included philosophy. You can import the logging library as follows:

```
import logging
```

Before getting into the programming part, you need to know something important—the level of logging. There are five levels of logging. These levels have priorities assigned to them. The following is the list of these levels in increasing order of severity:

```
DEBUG
INFO
WARNING
ERROR
CRITICAL
```

Now consider the code example in Listing 7-3.

Listing 7-3. prog02.py

```
import logging
logging.debug('Debug')
logging.info('Info')
logging.warning('Warning')
logging.error('Error')
logging.critical('Critical')
```

The output is as follows:

```
WARNING:root:Warning
ERROR:root:Error
CRITICAL:root:Critical
```

As you can see, only the last three log lines are printed. This is because the default level of logging is `Warning`. This means that all the levels of logging starting with `warning` will be logged. These include `Warning`, `Error`, and `Critical`.

You can change the level of logging, as shown in Listing 7-4.

Listing 7-4. prog03.py

```
import logging
logging.basicConfig(level=logging.DEBUG)
logging.debug('Debug')
logging.info('Info')
logging.warning('Warning')
logging.error('Error')
logging.critical('Critical')
```

As you can see, the `basicConfig()` routine configures the level of logging. You need to call this routine before calling any logging routines. This example sets the logging level to `Debug`. `Debug` is the lowest level of logging and this means that all the logs with logging level `Debug` and above will be recorded. The output is as follows:

```
DEBUG:root:Debug
INFO:root:Info
WARNING:root:Warning
ERROR:root:Error
CRITICAL:root:Critical
```

Let's look at the log messages in detail. As you can see, the log messages are divided into three parts. The first part is the level of the log. The second part is the name of the logger. In this case, it is the root logger. The third part is the string that you pass to the logging routines. You will learn later how to change the details of this message.

This is a good time to discuss what the different logging levels mean. Debug and Info levels usually indicate general execution of programs. The Warning logging level indicates problems that are not showstoppers. Error is used when you have serious problems affecting the normal execution of your programs. Finally, Critical is the highest level and it indicates a system-wide failure.

Logging to a File

You have learned how to display log messages to the terminal. You can also log messages to a file, as shown in Listing 7-5.

Listing 7-5. prog04.py

```
import logging
logging.basicConfig(filename='logfile.log',
                    encoding='utf-8',
                    level=logging.DEBUG)
logging.debug('Debug')
logging.info('Info')
logging.warning('Warning')
logging.error('Error')
logging.critical('Critical')
```

As you can see, the program sets the encoding and the name of the log file. Run the program and check the log file.

This program checks for the existence of the log file with the name passed as a string to the basicConfig() routine. If the file does not exist, it creates the file with the name. Otherwise, it appends to the existing file. If you want to create a fresh file every time you execute the code, you can do that using the code in Listing 7-6.

Listing 7-6. prog05.py

```python
import logging
logging.basicConfig(filename='logfile.log',
                    encoding='utf-8',
                    filemode='w',
                    level=logging.DEBUG)
logging.debug('Debug')
logging.info('Info')
logging.warning('Warning')
logging.error('Error')
logging.critical('Critical')
```

Notice the additional parameter and the associated argument for the call of the basicConfig() routine.

Customizing the Log Message

You can customize your log messages as well. You have to specify this by passing an argument to the parameter of the basicConfig() routine. Listing 7-7 shows an example.

Listing 7-7. prog06.py

```python
import logging
logging.basicConfig(filename='logfile.log',
                    format='%(asctime)s:%(levelname)s:%(message)s',
                    encoding='utf-8',
                    filemode='w',
                    level=logging.DEBUG)
logging.debug('Debug')
logging.info('Info')
```

```
logging.warning('Warning')
logging.error('Error')
logging.critical('Critical')
```

As you can see, this example passes the formatting string '%(asctime)s:%(levelname)s:%(message)s' to the parameter format of the basicConfig() routine. The output is as follows:

```
2021-09-02 13:36:35,401:DEBUG:Debug
2021-09-02 13:36:35,401:INFO:Info
2021-09-02 13:36:35,401:WARNING:Warning
2021-09-02 13:36:35,401:ERROR:Error
2021-09-02 13:36:35,401:CRITICAL:Critical
```

The output shows the date and time, the logging level, and the message.

Customizing Logging Operations

Up to now, the examples have been using the default logger, known as root. You can also create your own custom loggers. Logger objects send log messages to handler objects. Handlers send the log messages to their destinations. The destination can be a log file or the console. You can create objects for console handlers and file handlers. Log formatters are used to format the contents of the log messages. Let's look at an example line by line. Create a new file called prog07.py. You will now see how to add the code to this file to show customized logging operations.

Import the library as follows:

```
import logging
```

Create a custom logger as follows:

```
logger = logging.getLogger('myLogger')
logger.setLevel(logging.DEBUG)
```

You have created the custom logger with the name myLogger. Whenever you include the name in the log message, it will show myLogger in place of root. Now create a handler to log to a file.

```
fh = logging.FileHandler('mylog.log', encoding='utf-8')
fh.setLevel(logging.DEBUG)
```

Create a file formatter:

```
file_formatter = logging.Formatter('%(asctime)s - %(name)s - %(levelname)s - %(message)s')
```

Set it to the file handler:

```
fh.setFormatter(file_formatter)
```

Add the file handler to the logger:

```
logger.addHandler(fh)
```

You can create a console handler too. Repeat these steps for a new console handler:

```
ch = logging.StreamHandler()
ch.setLevel(logging.DEBUG)
console_formatter = logging.Formatter('%(asctime)s:%(name)s:%(levelname)s:%(message)s')
ch.setFormatter(console_formatter)
logger.addHandler(ch)
```

The entire script is shown in Listing 7-8.

Listing 7-8. prog07.py

```python
import logging
logger = logging.getLogger('myLogger')
logger.setLevel(logging.DEBUG)

fh = logging.FileHandler('mylog.log',
                         encoding='utf-8')
fh.setLevel(logging.DEBUG)
file_formatter = logging.Formatter('%(asctime)s - %(name)s -
%(levelname)s - %(message)s')
fh.setFormatter(file_formatter)
logger.addHandler(fh)
ch = logging.StreamHandler()
ch.setLevel(logging.DEBUG)
console_formatter = logging.Formatter('%(asctime)s:%(name)
s:%(levelname)s:%(message)s')
ch.setFormatter(console_formatter)
logger.addHandler(ch)
logger.debug('Debug')
logger.info('Info')
logger.warning('Warning')
logger.error('Error')
logger.critical('Critical')
```

This is how you can simultaneously log onto the console and onto a file. Run the code and see the output.

Rotating a Log File

You can also have rotating log file. You just need to change one line in Listing 7-8. Rotating log files means that all the new logs will be written to a new file and the old logs will be backed up by renaming the log files. Check out Listing 7-9.

Listing 7-9. prog08.py

```
import logging
import logging.handlers
logfile = 'mylog.log'
logger = logging.getLogger('myLogger')
logger.setLevel(logging.DEBUG)
rfh = logging.handlers.RotatingFileHandler(logfile,
                                    maxBytes=10,
                                    backupCount=5)
rfh.setLevel(logging.DEBUG)
file_formatter = logging.Formatter('%(asctime)s - %(name)s -
%(levelname)s - %(message)s')
rfh.setFormatter(file_formatter)
logger.addHandler(rfh)
ch = logging.StreamHandler()
ch.setLevel(logging.DEBUG)
console_formatter = logging.Formatter('%(asctime)s:%(name)
s:%(levelname)s:%(message)s')
ch.setFormatter(console_formatter)
logger.addHandler(ch)
logger.debug('Debug')
logger.info('Info')
logger.warning('Warning')
logger.error('Error')
logger.critical('Critical')
```

As you can see in Listing 7-9, the code has implemented the rotating file handle. The following line of code creates it:

```
rfh = logging.handlers.RotatingFileHandler(logfile,
                                           maxBytes=10,
                                           backupCount=5)
```

It creates log files as follows:

```
mylog.log
mylog.log.1
mylog.log.2
mylog.log.3
mylog.log.4
mylog.log.5
```

The most recent logs are saved in `mylog.log` and its capacity is 10 bytes. When this log file reaches 10 bytes, as specified in the routine call parameter `maxBytes`, it is renamed `mylog.log.1`. When the file is full again, this process repeats and `mylog.log.2` is renamed `mylog.log.2`. This process continues and the files from `mylog.log.5` onward are purged. This is because you passed 5 as an argument to the `backupCount` parameter. As an exercise, try changing the arguments.

Using Multiple Loggers

You can use multiple loggers in your programs as well. Listing 7-10 creates two loggers, one handler, and one formatter. The handler is shared between the loggers.

Listing 7-10. prog09.py

```
import logging
logger1 = logging.getLogger('Logger1')
logger1.setLevel(logging.DEBUG)
logger2 = logging.getLogger('Logger2')
logger2.setLevel(logging.DEBUG)
ch = logging.StreamHandler()
ch.setLevel(logging.DEBUG)
console_formatter = logging.Formatter('%(asctime)s:%(name)
s:%(levelname)s:%(message)s')
ch.setFormatter(console_formatter)
logger1.addHandler(ch)
logger2.addHandler(ch)
logger1.debug('Debug')
logger2.debug('Debug')
logger1.info('Info')
logger2.info('Info')
logger1.warning('Warning')
logger2.warning('Warning')
logger1.error('Error')
logger2.error('Error')
logger1.critical('Critical')
logger2.critical('Critical')
```

The output is as follows:

```
2021-09-03 00:25:40,135:Logger1:DEBUG:Debug
2021-09-03 00:25:40,153:Logger2:DEBUG:Debug
2021-09-03 00:25:40,161:Logger1:INFO:Info
2021-09-03 00:25:40,168:Logger2:INFO:Info
2021-09-03 00:25:40,176:Logger1:WARNING:Warning
2021-09-03 00:25:40,184:Logger2:WARNING:Warning
```

```
2021-09-03 00:25:40,193:Logger1:ERROR:Error
2021-09-03 00:25:40,200:Logger2:ERROR:Error
2021-09-03 00:25:40,224:Logger1:CRITICAL:Critical
2021-09-03 00:25:40,238:Logger2:CRITICAL:Critical
```

Now you'll see how to create separate handler and formatter for both loggers. Listing 7-11 shows an example.

Listing 7-11. prog10.py

```python
import logging
logger1 = logging.getLogger('Logger1')
logger1.setLevel(logging.DEBUG)
logger2 = logging.getLogger('Logger2')
logger2.setLevel(logging.DEBUG)
ch = logging.StreamHandler()
ch.setLevel(logging.DEBUG)
console_formatter = logging.Formatter('%(asctime)s:%(name)
s:%(levelname)s:%(message)s')
ch.setFormatter(console_formatter)
logger1.addHandler(ch)
fh = logging.FileHandler('mylog.log',
                            encoding='utf-8')
fh.setLevel(logging.DEBUG)
file_formatter = logging.Formatter('%(asctime)s - %(name)s -
%(levelname)s - %(message)s')
fh.setFormatter(file_formatter)
logger2.addHandler(fh)
logger1.debug('Debug')
logger2.debug('Debug')
logger1.info('Info')
logger2.info('Info')
logger1.warning('Warning')
```

```
logger2.warning('Warning')
logger1.error('Error')
logger2.error('Error')
logger1.critical('Critical')
logger2.critical('Critical')
```

As you can see, there are two separate sets of a logger, a handler, and a formatter. One set sends logs to the console and another set sends logs to a log file. The output to the console is as follows:

```
2021-09-03 15:13:37,513:Logger1:DEBUG:Debug
2021-09-03 15:13:37,533:Logger1:INFO:Info
2021-09-03 15:13:37,542:Logger1:WARNING:Warning
2021-09-03 15:13:37,552:Logger1:ERROR:Error
2021-09-03 15:13:37,560:Logger1:CRITICAL:Critical
```

The output to the log file is as follows:

```
2021-09-03 15:13:37,532 - Logger2 - DEBUG - Debug
2021-09-03 15:13:37,542 - Logger2 - INFO - Info
2021-09-03 15:13:37,551 - Logger2 - WARNING - Warning
2021-09-03 15:13:37,560 - Logger2 - ERROR - Error
2021-09-03 15:13:37,569 - Logger2 - CRITICAL – Critical
```

Logging with Threads

Sometimes, you'll use multithreading in your programs. Python allows you to use the logging feature with threads. This ensures that you are informed about the details of execution of threads you use in your programs. Create a new Python file and name it prog11.py. Add the following code to that file:

```
import logging
import threading
import time
```

Now create a function as follows:

```
def worker(arg, number):
    while not arg['stop']:
        logging.debug('Hello from worker() thread number '
                        + str(number))
        time.sleep(0.75 * number)
```

This function accepts an argument and, unless you terminate it, it keeps running a loop displaying a message.

Let's configure the default console logger as follows:

```
logging.basicConfig(level='DEBUG',
format='%(asctime)s:%(name)s:%(levelname)s:%(message)s')
```

Now create two threads as follows:

```
info = {'stop': False}
thread1 = threading.Thread(target=worker, args=(info, 1, ))
thread1.start()
thread2 = threading.Thread(target=worker, args=(info, 2, ))
thread2.start()
```

Create a loop that will be interrupted by the keyboard and will also interrupt the threads:

```
while True:
    try:
        logging.debug('Hello from the main() thread')
        time.sleep(1)
    except KeyboardInterrupt:
        info['stop'] = True
        break
```

Finally, join these threads:

```
thread1.join()
thread2.join()
```

The entire program is shown in Listing 7-12.

Listing 7-12. prog11.py

```
import logging
import threading
import time
def worker(arg, number):
    while not arg['stop']:
        logging.debug('Hello from worker() thread number '
                        + str(number))
        time.sleep(0.75 * number)
logging.basicConfig(level='DEBUG',
format='%(asctime)s:%(name)s:%(levelname)s:%(message)s')
info = {'stop': False}
thread1 = threading.Thread(target=worker, args=(info, 1, ))
thread1.start()
thread2 = threading.Thread(target=worker, args=(info, 2, ))
thread2.start()
while True:
    try:
        logging.debug('Hello from the main() thread')
        time.sleep(1)
    except KeyboardInterrupt:
        info['stop'] = True
        break
thread1.join()
thread2.join()
```

Run the program and then press Ctrl+C to terminate it after a few seconds. The output is as follows:

```
2021-09-03 15:34:27,071:root:DEBUG:Hello from worker() thread
number 1
2021-09-03 15:34:27,304:root:DEBUG:Hello from the main() thread
2021-09-03 15:34:27,664:root:DEBUG:Hello from worker() thread
number 2
2021-09-03 15:34:27,851:root:DEBUG:Hello from worker() thread
number 1
2021-09-03 15:34:28,364:root:DEBUG:Hello from the main() thread
2021-09-03 15:34:28,629:root:DEBUG:Hello from worker() thread
number 1
2021-09-03 15:34:29,239:root:DEBUG:Hello from worker() thread
number 2
2021-09-03 15:34:29,381:root:DEBUG:Hello from the main() thread
2021-09-03 15:34:29,414:root:DEBUG:Hello from worker() thread
number 1
2021-09-03 15:34:30,205:root:DEBUG:Hello from worker() thread
number 1
2021-09-03 15:34:30,444:root:DEBUG:Hello from the main() thread
2021-09-03 15:34:30,788:root:DEBUG:Hello from worker() thread
number 2
2021-09-03 15:34:30,990:root:DEBUG:Hello from worker() thread
number 1
2021-09-03 15:34:31,503:root:DEBUG:Hello from the main() thread
2021-09-03 15:34:31,828:root:DEBUG:Hello from worker() thread
number 1
2021-09-03 15:34:32,311:root:DEBUG:Hello from worker() thread
number 2
2021-09-03 15:34:32,574:root:DEBUG:Hello from the main() thread
```

```
2021-09-03 15:34:32,606:root:DEBUG:Hello from worker() thread
number 1
2021-09-03 15:34:33,400:root:DEBUG:Hello from worker() thread
number 1
2021-09-03 15:34:33,634:root:DEBUG:Hello from the main() thread
2021-09-03 15:34:33,865:root:DEBUG:Hello from worker() thread
number 2
2021-09-03 15:34:34,175:root:DEBUG:Hello from worker() thread
number 1
2021-09-03 15:34:34,688:root:DEBUG:Hello from the main() thread
2021-09-03 15:34:34,969:root:DEBUG:Hello from worker() thread
number 1
2021-09-03 15:34:35,456:root:DEBUG:Hello from worker() thread
number 2
Traceback (most recent call last):
  File "C:/Users/Ashwin/Google Drive/Python Unit Test
Automation - Second Edition/Code/Chapter07/prog11.py", line 26,
in <module>
    thread2.join()
KeyboardInterrupt
```

Multiple Loggers Writing to the Same Target

You can have multiple loggers writing to the same target. The code example shown in Listing 7-13 sends the logs of two different loggers to a console handler and a file handler.

Listing 7-13. prog12.py

```python
import logging
logger1 = logging.getLogger('Logger1')
logger1.setLevel(logging.DEBUG)
logger2 = logging.getLogger('Logger2')
logger2.setLevel(logging.DEBUG)
ch = logging.StreamHandler()
ch.setLevel(logging.DEBUG)
console_formatter = logging.Formatter('%(asctime)s:%(name)
s:%(levelname)s:%(message)s')
ch.setFormatter(console_formatter)
logger1.addHandler(ch)
logger2.addHandler(ch)
fh = logging.FileHandler('mylog.log',
                         encoding='utf-8')
fh.setLevel(logging.DEBUG)
file_formatter = logging.Formatter('%(asctime)s - %(name)s -
%(levelname)s - %(message)s')
fh.setFormatter(file_formatter)
logger1.addHandler(fh)
logger2.addHandler(fh)
logger1.debug('Debug')
logger2.debug('Debug')
logger1.info('Info')
logger2.info('Info')
logger1.warning('Warning')
logger2.warning('Warning')
logger1.error('Error')
logger2.error('Error')
logger1.critical('Critical')
logger2.critical('Critical')
```

Run the program to see the following output on the console:

```
2021-09-03 16:10:53,938:Logger1:DEBUG:Debug
2021-09-03 16:10:53,956:Logger2:DEBUG:Debug
2021-09-03 16:10:53,966:Logger1:INFO:Info
2021-09-03 16:10:53,974:Logger2:INFO:Info
2021-09-03 16:10:53,983:Logger1:WARNING:Warning
2021-09-03 16:10:53,993:Logger2:WARNING:Warning
2021-09-03 16:10:54,002:Logger1:ERROR:Error
2021-09-03 16:10:54,011:Logger2:ERROR:Error
2021-09-03 16:10:54,031:Logger1:CRITICAL:Critical
2021-09-03 16:10:54,049:Logger2:CRITICAL:Critical
```

The log file contains the following log after the execution of the program:

```
2021-09-03 16:10:53,938 - Logger1 - DEBUG - Debug
2021-09-03 16:10:53,956 - Logger2 - DEBUG - Debug
2021-09-03 16:10:53,966 - Logger1 - INFO - Info
2021-09-03 16:10:53,974 - Logger2 - INFO - Info
2021-09-03 16:10:53,983 - Logger1 - WARNING - Warning
2021-09-03 16:10:53,993 - Logger2 - WARNING - Warning
2021-09-03 16:10:54,002 - Logger1 - ERROR - Error
2021-09-03 16:10:54,011 - Logger2 - ERROR - Error
2021-09-03 16:10:54,031 - Logger1 - CRITICAL - Critical
2021-09-03 16:10:54,049 - Logger2 - CRITICAL – Critical
```

Logging with loguru

There is another logging mechanism for Python that can be installed and used. It is known as loguru. It is a third-party library, so it needs to be installed separately. It is slightly better than the built-in logger and has more features. In this section, you see how to install it, use it, and explore it.

You can install loguru on Windows and Linux using the following command:

```
pip3 install loguru
```

The following is the installation log on a Windows computer:

```
Collecting loguru
  Downloading loguru-0.5.3-py3-none-any.whl (57 kB)
     |███████████████████████████████| 57 kB 1.1 MB/s
Collecting win32-setctime>=1.0.0
  Downloading win32_setctime-1.0.3-py3-none-any.whl (3.5 kB)
Requirement already satisfied: colorama>=0.3.4 in c:\users\
ashwin\appdata\local\programs\python\python39\lib\site-packages
(from loguru) (0.4.4)
Installing collected packages: win32-setctime, loguru
Successfully installed loguru-0.5.3 win32-setctime-1.0.3
```

Using loguru and the Available Logging Levels

There is only one logger in loguru. You can configure it per your needs. By default, it sends the log messages to stderr. Listing 7-14 shows a simple example.

Listing 7-14. Prog13.py

```
from loguru import logger
logger.trace('Trace')
logger.debug('Debug')
logger.info('Info')
logger.success('Success')
logger.warning('Warning')
logger.error('Error')
logger.critical('Critical')
```

The code in Listing 7-14 lists all the logging levels in increasing order of severity. You can also log everything to a file, as shown in Listing 7-15.

Listing 7-15. Prog14.py

```
from loguru import logger
import sys
logger.add("mylog_{time}.log",
           format="{time}:{level}:{message}",
           level="TRACE")
logger.trace('Trace')
logger.debug('Debug')
logger.info('Info')
logger.success('Success')
logger.warning('Warning')
logger.error('Error')
logger.critical('Critical')
```

When you run this, the output to the file is as follows:

```
2021-09-02T21:56:04.677854+0530:TRACE:Trace
2021-09-02T21:56:04.680839+0530:DEBUG:Debug
2021-09-02T21:56:04.706743+0530:INFO:Info
```

```
2021-09-02T21:56:04.726689+0530:SUCCESS:Success
2021-09-02T21:56:04.749656+0530:WARNING:Warning
2021-09-02T21:56:04.778333+0530:ERROR:Error
2021-09-02T21:56:04.802271+0530:CRITICAL:Critical
```

You can also create a custom log level, as shown in Listing 7-16.

Listing 7-16. Prog15.py

```
from loguru import logger
import sys
logger.add("mylog_{time}.log",
            format="{time}:{level}:{message}",
            level="TRACE")
new_level = logger.level("OKAY", no=15, color="<green>")
logger.trace('Trace')
logger.debug('Debug')
logger.log("OKAY", "All is OK!")
logger.info('Info')
```

This code creates a new level with the logger.level() routine. You can use it with the logger.log() routine. Run the program. The output dumped in the log file is as follows:

```
2021-09-02T22:44:59.834885+0530:TRACE:Trace
2021-09-02T22:44:59.839871+0530:DEBUG:Debug
2021-09-02T22:44:59.893727+0530:OKAY:All is OK!
2021-09-02T22:44:59.945590+0530:INFO:Info
```

Customizing File Retention

Log files, just like any other piece of information, require storage space. Over time and multiple execution passes, the log files can grow bigger and bigger. Nowadays, storage is cheaper. Even so, there are always limitations to space and storing older and unnecessary logs is a waste of space. Many organizations have policies in place for retaining older logs. You can implement those policies in the following way.

The following configuration rotates big files. You can specify the size of the file as follows:

```
logger.add("mylog_{time}.log", rotation="2 MB")
```

The following configuration creates a new file after midnight:

```
logger.add("mylog_{time}.log", rotation="00:01")
```

The following configuration rotates week-old files:

```
logger.add("mylog_{time}.log", rotation="1 week")
```

The following configuration cleans up a file after a specified number of days:

```
logger.add("mylog_{time}.log", retention="5 days")  # Cleanup
after some time
```

The following configuration compresses the files into the ZIP format:

```
logger.add("mylog_{time}.log", compression="zip")
```

As an exercise, try all these configurations.

Customizing Tracing

You can customize the tracing process and obtain detailed information about any underlying problems. It is difficult to implement this in the built-in logger, but it can be easily done using loguru. You can customize tracing by passing some additional arguments, as shown in Listing 7-17.

Listing 7-17. Prog16.py

```python
from loguru import logger

logger.add('mylog.log',
           backtrace=True,
           diagnose=True)

def function1(a, b):
    return a / b

def function2(c):
    try:
        function1(5, c)
    except ZeroDivisionError:
        logger.exception('Divide by Zero!')

function2(0)
```

These additional parameters allow you to trace failures in detail. The log file has the following output:

```
2021-09-03 17:16:40.122 | ERROR    |
__main__:function2:14 - Divide by Zero!
Traceback (most recent call last):

  File "<string>", line 1, in <module>
```

```
File "C:\Users\Ashwin\AppData\Local\Programs\Python\Python39\
lib\idlelib\run.py", line 156, in main
  ret = method(*args, **kwargs)
            |        |      -> {}
            |        -> (<code object <module> at
         0x000001D3E9EFDB30, file
         "C:/Users/Ashwin/Google Drive/Python Unit Test
         Automation - Second Edition...
         -> <bound method Executive.runcode of <idlelib.run.
         Executive object at 0x000001D3E802F730>>

File "C:\Users\Ashwin\AppData\Local\Programs\Python\Python39\
lib\idlelib\run.py", line 559, in runcode
  exec(code, self.locals)
         |      |    -> {'__name__': '__main__', '__doc__':
None, '__package__': None, '__loader__': <class '_frozen_
importlib.BuiltinImporter'>, '__...
         |      -> <idlelib.run.Executive object at
0x000001D3E802F730>
         -> <code object <module> at 0x000001D3E9EFDB30,
         file "C:/Users/Ashwin/Google Drive/Python Unit Test
         Automation - Second Edition/...

File "C:/Users/Ashwin/Google Drive/Python Unit Test
Automation - Second Edition/Code/Chapter07/prog16.py",
line 16, in <module>
  function2(0)
  -> <function function2 at 0x000001D3EA6264C0>

> File "C:/Users/Ashwin/Google Drive/Python Unit Test
Automation - Second Edition/Code/Chapter07/prog16.py", line 12,
in function2
```

```
function1(5, c)
|              -> 0
-> <function function1 at 0x000001D3EA61DE50>
```

```
File "C:/Users/Ashwin/Google Drive/Python Unit Test
Automation - Second Edition/Code/Chapter07/prog16.py",
line 8, in function1
   return a / b
          |   -> 0
          -> 5
```

```
ZeroDivisionError: division by zero
```

Customizing the Log Message Format and Display

You can also customize the log message format and determine how it is displayed on the console, as shown in Listing 7-18.

Listing 7-18. Prog17.py

```python
from loguru import logger
import sys
logger.add(sys.stdout,
        colorize=True,
        format="<blue>{time}</blue> <level>{message}
        </level>")
logger.add('mylog.log',
        format="{time:YYYY-MM-DD @ HH:mm:ss} - {level} -
        {message}")
logger.debug('Debug')
logger.info('Info')
```

If you run this on the console, you will get the output shown in Figure 7-1.

```
2021-09-03 17:35:28.996 |                    |    main   :<module>:11 -

2021-09-03 17:35:29.006 | INFO     |    main   :<module>:12 - Info
                                        Info
```

Figure 7-1. *Customized output*

Configuring with a Dictionary

You can configure the log files with a dictionary as well, as shown in Listing 7-19.

Listing 7-19. Prog18.py

```python
from loguru import logger
import sys
config = {
    'handlers': [
        {'sink': sys.stdout, 'format': '{time} - {message}'},
        {'sink': 'mylog.log', 'serialize': True}]
}
logger.configure(**config)
logger.debug('Debug')
logger.info('Info')
```

Run the program and you will see the following output:

```
2021-09-03T17:44:49.396318+0530 - Debug
2021-09-03T17:44:49.416051+0530 - Info
```

Conclusion

This chapter explained Python's logging mechanisms in detail. Logging is a very useful technique used to analyze problems encountered during the execution of programs. Every application or program has unique requirements for logging and you can include diverse and detailed information in the log files. The chapter covered a few examples of logging. As an exercise, identify what kind of information you want to see in the logs in your Python programs and then write the appropriate code for logging.

The next chapter is the culmination of all that you have learned throughout this book. You learn about TDD (test-driven development).

CHAPTER 8

Tips and Tricks

In the first chapter of this book, you about learned the history and philosophy of Python. Subsequent chapters explored the features of various test automation frameworks in Python. The frameworks you explored included `doctest`, `unittest`, `nose`, `nose2`, and `pytest`. Later, you learned about Selenium and logging in detail. This chapter looks at coding conventions that will make the test discovery easier across these frameworks. Then, you will look at the concept of *test-driven development* and learn how it can be implemented in Python 3 projects with the help of `pytest`.

Coding and Filenaming Conventions for Easier Test Discovery

You have seen that all the `xUnit`-style frameworks include test discovery, that is, the automated detection, execution, and report generation of tests. This is a very important feature, as it makes life easier for code testers. You can even schedule the test discovery process using OS schedulers (for example, `cron` in Linux-based operating systems and Windows Scheduler in Windows), and they will automatically run tests at scheduled times.

© Ashwin Pajankar 2022
A. Pajankar, *Python Unit Test Automation*, https://doi.org/10.1007/978-1-4842-7854-3_8

In order to ensure that the test discovery system detects all the tests successfully, I usually follow these code and filename conventions:

- The names of all the test modules (the test files) should start with test_

- The names of all the test functions should start with test_

- The names of all the test classes should start with Test

- The names of all the test methods should start with test_

- Group all the tests into test classes and packages

- All the packages with test code should have an init.py file

It is always a good idea to follow the PEP 8 convention for the code. It can be found at https://www.python.org/dev/peps/pep-0008/.

If you use these conventions for your code and filenames, the test discovery feature of all the test automation frameworks—including unittest, nose, nose2, and pytest—will detect the tests without any problem. So, the next time you write your tests, follow these conventions for best results.

Note   You can read more about xUnit at https://www.martinfowler.com/bliki/Xunit.html and http://xunitpatterns.com/

Test-Driven Development with pytest

Test-driven development (TDD) is a paradigm whereby you implement a new feature or requirement by writing tests first, watch them fail, and then write the code to make the failed tests pass. Once the basic skeleton is implemented this way, you then build on this by altering the tests and changing the development code to accommodate the added functionality. You repeat this process as many times as needed to accommodate all new requirements.

Essentially, TDD is a cycle where you write the tests first, watch them fail, implement the required features, and repeat this process until the new features are added to the existing code.

By writing the automated tests before the development code, it forces you to think about the problem at hand first. As you start to build your tests, you have to think about the way you write the development code that must pass the already-written automated tests in order to be accepted.

Figure 8-1 sums up the TDD approach.

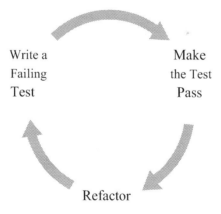

Figure 8-1. TDD flow

To see how TDD is implemented in Python with pytest, create a directory called chapter08 for this TDD in the code directory. You will use this directory for the TDD exercise.

Create the test module shown in Listing 8-1 in the chapter08 directory.

Listing 8-1. test_module01.py

```python
class TestClass01:

    def test_case01(self):
        calc = Calculator()
        result = calc.add(2, 2)
        assert 4 == result
```

Run the code in Listing 8-1 with the following command:

```
py.test -vs test_module01.py
```

The output will be as follows:

```
===================== test session starts =====================
platform linux -- Python 3.4.2, pytest-3.0.4, py-1.4.31,
pluggy-0.4.0 -- / usr/bin/python3
cachedir: .cache
rootdir: /home/pi/book/code/chapter08,
inifile:
collected 1 items

test_module01.py::TestClass01::test_case01 FAILED
=========================== FAILURES ===========================
_____ TestClass01.test_case01_____

self = <test_module01.TestClass01 object at 0x763c03b0>
```

```
    def test_case01(self):
>       calc = Calculator()
E       NameError: name 'Calculator' is not defined

test_module01.py:4: NameError
==================== 1 failed in 0.29 seconds =================
```

From this output, you can see that the problem is that Calculator has not been imported. That is because you have not created the Calculator module! So let's define the Calculator module in a file called calculator. py, as shown in Listing 8-2, in the same directory.

Listing 8-2. calculator.py

```
class Calculator:

    def add(self, x, y):
        pass
```

Make sure that there are no errors in calculator.py by running the following command every time you modify the module:

```
python3 calculator.py
```

Now import Calculator in the test module, as shown in Listing 8-3.

Listing 8-3. test_module01.py

```
from calculator import Calculator class TestClass01:
def test_case01(self):
calc = Calculator() result = calc.add(2, 2) assert 4 == result
```

Run the test_module01.py again. The output will be as follows:

```
==================== test session starts ====================
platform linux -- Python 3.4.2, pytest-3.0.4, py-1.4.31,
pluggy-0.4.0 --
```

197

```
/usr/bin/python3
cachedir: .cache
rootdir: /home/pi/book/code/chapter08,
inifile:
collected 1 items

test_module01.py::TestClass01::test_case01 FAILED
========================= FAILURES ==============================
_____ TestClass01.test_case01_____

self = <test_module01.TestClass01 object at 0x762c24b0>

   def test_case01(self):
      calc = Calculator()
      result = calc.add(2, 2)
>     assert 4 == result
E     assert 4 == None

test_module01.py:9: AssertionError
=================== 1 failed in 0.32 seconds ==================
```

The add() method returns the wrong value (i.e., pass), as it does not do anything at the moment. Fortunately, pytest returns the line with the error in the test run so you can decide what you need to change. Let's fix the code in the add() method in calculator.py, as shown in Listing 8-4.

Listing 8-4. calculator.py

```
class Calculator:

   def add(self, x, y):
      return x+y
```

You can run the test module again. Here is the output:

```
===================== test session starts =====================
platform linux -- Python 3.4.2, pytest-3.0.4, py-1.4.31,
pluggy-0.4.0 --
/usr/bin/python3
cachedir: .cache
rootdir: /home/pi/book/code/chapter08,
inifile:
collected 1 items

test_module01.py::TestClass01::test_case01 PASSED
================== 1 passed in 0.08 seconds ==================
```

Now you can add more test cases to the test module (as shown in Listing 8-5) to check for more features.

Listing 8-5. test_module01.py

```python
from calculator import Calculator
import pytest

    class TestClass01:

        def test_case01(self):
            calc = Calculator()
            result = calc.add(2, 2)
            assert 4 == result

        def test_case02(self):
            with pytest.raises(ValueError):
                result = Calculator().add(2, 'two')
```

The modified code shown in Listing 8-5 is trying to add an integer and a string, which should raise a ValueError exception.

If you run the modified test module, you get the following:

```
==================== test session starts ====================
platform linux -- Python 3.4.2, pytest-3.0.4, py-1.4.31,
pluggy-0.4.0 -- / usr/bin/python3
cachedir: .cache
rootdir: /home/pi/book/code/chapter08,
inifile:
collected 2 items

test_module01.py::TestClass01::test_case01 PASSED test_
module01.py::TestClass01::test_case02 FAILED


======================== FAILURES ===========================
_____ TestClass01.test_case02_____

self = <test_module01.TestClass01 object at 0x7636f050>

    def test_case02(self):
        with pytest.raises(ValueError):
>           result = Calculator().add(2, 'two')

test_module01.py:14:

_ _ _ _ _ _ _ _ _ _ _ _ _ _ _ _ _ _ _ _ _ _ _ _ _ _ _ _ _
self = <calculator.Calculator object at 0x7636faf0>, x = 2,
y = 'two'
    def add(self, x, y):
>       return x+y
E       TypeError: unsupported operand type(s) for +: 'int'
and 'str'

calculator.py:4: TypeError
============= 1 failed, 1 passed in 0.33 seconds ============
```

As you can see in the output, the second test fails because it does not detect a ValueError exception. So, let's add the provision to check if both the arguments are numeric, or otherwise raise a ValueError exception—see Listing 8-6.

Listing 8-6. calculator.py

```
class Calculator:

    def add(self, x, y):
        number_types = (int, float, complex)

            if isinstance(x, number_types) and isinstance(y,
            number_types):
                return x + y
        else:
            raise ValueError
```

Finally, Listing 8-7 shows how to add two more test cases to the test module to check if add() is behaving as expected.

Listing 8-7. test_module01.py

```
from calculator import Calculator
import pytest

class TestClass01:

    def test_case01(self):
        calc = Calculator()
        result = calc.add(2, 2)
        assert 4 == result

    def test_case02(self):
        with pytest.raises(ValueError):
            result = Calculator().add(2, 'two')
```

```
    def test_case03(self):
        with pytest.raises(ValueError):
            result = Calculator().add('two', 2)

    def test_case04(self):
        with pytest.raises(ValueError):
            result = Calculator().add('two', 'two')
```

When you run the test module in Listing 8-7, you get the
following output:

```
====================== test session starts ======================
platform linux -- Python 3.4.2, pytest-3.0.4, py-1.4.31,
pluggy-0.4.0 -- / usr/bin/python3
cachedir: .cache
rootdir: /home/pi/book/code/chapter08,
inifile:
collected 4 items

test_module01.py::TestClass01::test_case01 PASSED test_
module01.py::TestClass01::test_case02 PASSED test_module01.
py::TestClass01::test_case03 PASSED test_module01.
py::TestClass01::test_case04 PASSED

=============== 4 passed in 0.14 seconds ================
```

This is how TDD is implemented in real-life projects. You write a failing
test first, refactor the development code, and continue with the same
process until the test passes. When you want to add a new feature, you
repeat this process to implement it.

Conclusion

In this chapter, you learned the coding and filename conventions for easy test discovery; these conventions can be implemented across all the automation frameworks. You also read a brief introduction to TDD.

This book began with an introduction to Python, including how to install it on the various OSs and the differences between Python versions 2 and version 3. Subsequent chapters explored the most commonly used test automation frameworks for Python.

Chapter 2 explored docstrings and explained how they are useful in writing doctests.

You learned that the doctest is not a very powerful test framework, as it lacks many essentials of a true test framework.

In Chapter 3, you were introduced to Python's batteries-included test automation framework, unittest. You learned how to write xUnit-style test cases for Python with unittest.

In Chapter 4, you explored a more advanced, but defunct, test automation framework called nose. You learned about the advanced features and plugins offered by nose. Because nose is not under active development, the chapter used nose2 as a test-runner for running nose and unittest tests.

In Chapter 5, you studied and explored one of the best unit test automation frameworks for Python, pytest. You learned how and why it is better than unittest and nose. You also explored its plugins and modular fixtures.

In Chapter 6, you studied and explored the Selenium browser automation framework, which is very useful in automating test cases for various web-related programming using web browsers.

Chapter 7 explored logging with logger and loguru. Logging is a very useful feature for developers and testers.

You have practiced numerous examples throughout the book, the goal of which is to instill you with confidence in Python test automation. You also learned to work with codebases where they have implemented test automation with `unittest`, `doctest`, or `nose` and plan a migration to `pytest`. You can now write your own routines and use logging to log the errors. You can also automate web-related test cases. Also, if you are a career Python developer or an automation expert, you can follow the TDD approach in your projects. I hope you have enjoyed reading this book as much as I enjoyed writing it. Happy Pythoning and testing!!

Index

A, B, C

D, E

F, G, H

I, J, K

Printed in the United States
by Baker & Taylor Publisher Services